To Peter
with :

CONFRONTING
THE PARANORMAL
– *A Christian Perspective* –

William H. Lendrum

(Foreword by Brother David Jardine)

William H. Lendrum

DEDICATION

To my wife Leah who has been my faithful companion in ministry for almost half a century.

THANKS

I am grateful to those who have encouraged me to write this book and who have accompanied and assisted me in ministry for many years. In particular, I acknowledge my debt to George and Molly Kerr, Alex and Joan Weir and the Reverend Brother David Jardine. They have been my willing helpers in ministry on many occasions and in various circumstances. My wife Leah has proof-read the full text and has made valuable suggestions by way of correction and clarification. My daughter Gillian has spent many hours typing the full manuscript and deserves the fullest praise for her work so willingly given. Without all these people this book would not have been written.

W.H.L.

Foreword
by Brother David Jardine SSF

I am delighted that Canon William Lendrum has put down on paper much of the knowledge that he has gleaned over many years about the deliverance ministry. For some time I have been convinced that he is one of the best men in the Church in Ireland in this branch of the ministry. It has been my privilege to join him on numerous occasions when he has been called to deal with paranormal activity in either people or places. I remember going with him to a home in East Belfast where the figure of a woman was appearing at night in the room of a little ten year old girl. This was very frightening for her. Billy came in, asked some questions, summed up the situation and dealt with it with great authority. That figure of the woman has never again appeared in that home. Every time I have joined Billy in exercising the ministry of deliverance he has operated with that same authority and effectiveness.

This book is well-written, informative and balanced. Billy explores every natural avenue before coming to the conclusion that there is a need for a deliverance ministry. His style is down to earth and easy to read. He deals with many aspects of the paranormal, and everything is backed up by scripture and personal experience.

This book will be very helpful to any who wish to be better informed about a Christian approach to the paranormal. It also gives good clear advice to those who may have to deal with it in the course of their ministry.

This is certainly the best book that I have read on the deliverance ministry for a very long time.

Contents

Introduction

It is with some reluctance that I put down on paper what I have witnessed during the past thirty years of Christian Ministry to those troubled by the paranormal. My reasons for doing so are four-fold.

First, it has been urged upon me by some friends that I make my experiences known to those who are interested in paranormal activity and who believe that there is a need to be met in that field today, a need that can and should be met by the Ministry of the Church. If people cannot find an answer to the problems, difficulties and fears thrown up by the outward manifestation of spiritual activity, which is both unsought and undesirable, where can that answer be found? Surely it is part of the gospel message that the risen Lord proclaimed,

"All authority in heaven and on earth has been given to me."
(Matthew 28 v.18)

Jesus has still that authority today. It is because he has given that authority to his Church that we can claim total victory over all the power of the enemy.

Second, it is my earnest desire that some will be encouraged to exercise this ministry when they come face to face with the need to do so. I recognise that there is always a danger that some enthusiastic and well meaning people will be drawn into this work and may do more harm than good. That is why the *leaders* of the main churches must take that risk. If they do not, who will? Some needy persons have sought help from mediums and clairvoyants because there has been no other to whom they can go. Others have gone to "spiritualist churches" because they could find no help in their own. It is very important that men and women in positions of authority and leadership in the Church, should know how to comfort, counsel and deliver those who find themselves disturbed, distressed or afflicted by something they cannot understand and that causes terrible dread or fear.

Third, I hope to show that some of the suffering that afflicts people, even in this 21st Century, has spiritual roots. The medical profession has taken enormous strides forward in the alleviation of pain and suffering. I have nothing but the highest admiration and praise for the dedication, discipline, knowledge and skill of surgeons, doctors, nurses and all involved in the work of healing but the Church also has a part to play. There are sicknesses and diseases that are grounded in the spiritual side of man's nature and require spiritual ministrations. They will not respond to material or psychiatric medicine. They require the authority and power of Jesus Christ to deliver them and set them free.

Fourth, I would contend that the turning away from God by the masses in western society has made natural man vulnerable to attacks by spiritual forces in society. Whilst modern man with his scientific world view has grasped the simple truth that every effect has its cause, he has failed to appreciate that there are also spiritual causes at work, that impinge on his life and produce deadly results. Those *spiritual* forces that mar people's lives are called demons or spirits in the New Testament. If they existed in our Lord's day, it is reasonable to suppose that they exist today. We need to know how to deal with them. That is why this book has been written. It is not a scholarly treatise on the general subject of the paranormal but an attempt by a plain man to share with those who are interested, some of his personal experiences as he has sought to serve God in the ministry of the Church of Ireland.

It is not my intention to promote the sensational or arouse the curiosity of those who take an unhealthy interest in paranormal activity. That would be an unworthy object. All that I have tried to do is to tell my story. This book is about some things that have happened to me.

Part 1 - The Reality of the Paranormal

Obviously some readers (including a few clergy) will have serious doubts about the reality of the paranormal. Living in western Europe with its scientific world view influences how we think about these things. Some will have difficulties accepting reports of the paranormal. They will look for a natural cause to explain some of the strange things that are described **and they are right in doing so.** I commend that approach. If we can find a satisfactory explanation for what occurs, that is the correct way to go. We should not attribute any occurence to paranormal activity if a more rational and natural explanation can be found.

Nevertheless, we should not be blindly dismissive of the possibility that an event may have an un-natural or supernatural cause. I hope to show in Part 1 from my personal experience over many years, that there are occasions when the balance of seeking the cause of strange and mysterious happenings is heavily and irresistably tilted towards the supernatural. Paranormal activity is real.

Chapter One
How It Began

My background, accomplishments and ministry in the Church are in the category of the ordinary and commonplace. I make no claim to any special favours or unusual gifts.

I was born in what was known in Belfast in the twenties as a kitchen house in the parish of Willowfield, in East Belfast. I had no outstanding qualities. My parents encouraged me to apply myself diligently to my school work at Park Parade Public Elementary School. They were good people, ambitious for me as parents are for their children. I was competitive by nature, so I was usually up among the front runners in a very ordinary academic field. Like many boys who had the good fortune to live near the Ormeau Park Playing Fields, that spirit of competitiveness found expression, perhaps too often, in football in the winter and cricket in the summer, frequently playing long after the park's closing time to the point where we could no longer see the ball. Happy days!

In those times, holidays meant spending a week or a fortnight in Bangor or Newcastle for those who were lucky. Many were not so fortunate. I was more blessed than most because I was privileged to spend four weeks annually in Co. Fermanagh with my maternal grandmother and her family. That may not sound a big deal to present generations of young people but for us it was like going to the other side of the world. It was a journey that involved changing trains at Omagh and Bundoran Junction to Irvinestown followed by a jaunt in a taxi to a cottage without running water or electricity or gas. That journey of five hours brought us to a place where food was cooked over a large turf fire set on a stone flagged floor under a huge chimney. I can still recollect the appetising smell of fried bacon and egg, the warmth of the welcome, the chickens wandering about and pecking for food outside the door, the green fields as far as the eye could see, the silence of the countryside. There was no television, no radio, no telephone and no newspapers. It was a different world.

For a young boy brought up in Belfast it was all very strange. At times there was little to do, especially when it rained and it did that often in Fermanagh. The word "boring" was not much in use in those days. Haymaking was good fun. Transporting water or wood using a donkey and cart was a delight. Social visiting was very acceptable when my sister and I were introduced as "cuddy" and "cub"(the Fermanagh words for boy and girl) and provided with good things to eat and drink.

However, the thing that I remember most clearly about my Fermanagh holidays was what Fermanagh people called a "ceilidh" (pronounced keili). At nightfall, people (usually unmarried men of which there were plenty in Fermanagh) would drop in for a chat. Looking back I am wondering why they came. Had it something to do with finding entertainment, chatting to the people from Belfast? Or had it something to do with the presence of two of my aunts who were eligible in those days? Whatever the reason, we looked forward to their arrival after the day's work in the fields was over.

They would sit around a large turf or wood fire in the light of paraffin oil lamps, smoke their pipes and swap stories about all kinds of things from the state of the crops to the latest news from town. Inevitably, someone would introduce ghost stories into the conversation. "John, tell that story about what you saw at the cross-roads." Things would take off from there. The Fermanagh man of those days was a good story-teller. His grammar was not the best (rather like that of Mark Twain's Huckleberry Finn) but he got the message across. He had plenty of practice in days when social intercourse was not replaced by television.

The result was that I believed what I heard and was convinced that of all the counties in Ireland, Fermanagh was well ahead in the ghost stakes. I was quite terrified at the very thought of going out alone after dark. I longed for the street lights of Belfast. What I did not understand was the Fermanagh man's sense of humour. These jokers of West Fermanagh were delighted to frighten the wits out of us clever, unsuspecting people from the big city!

I discovered later in life that most of those ghost stories originated in the imagination of some frightened soul in days gone by and had lost nothing in the telling over the years. It is important to keep that in mind. A healthy degree of scepticism is justified when we are confronted with stories that defy explanation. At the same time, we need to consider the wise and discerning words that William Shakespeare put into the mouth of Hamlet: "There are more things in heaven and earth, Horatio, than are dreamt of in your philosophy."

Most of the stories that I will tell in this book will be ones that I have personally investigated. By its very nature the subject of this book can never be presented as an exact science. We can no more prove the existence of ghosts or spirits by scientific methods than we can write QED after a carefully reasoned argument proving the existence of God. Nevertheless, there is enough evidence in many ghost stories to indicate that there are more things behind the facade of life on earth than we think or imagine.

Writing of my experiences in Fermanagh brings to my remembrance a ghost story that I heard when I was about twelve years of age. The events took place in Fermanagh but I heard the story when I was in Belfast. A play was presented on the radio called "The Coonian Ghost." By mere chance I happened to be listening and I can remember clearly to this day the things I heard and the powerful impression made on me. The story was centred on a farmhouse in Fermanagh where strange and frightening things took place. As I have looked back at the details of that story over the years, I thought that perhaps the author of the play had taken liberties and had added details to the story to give it a greater effect. Recently I received a detailed account of what happened in a book by the Coonian History Group called "Road to the Hills". One chapter dealt with the Coonian Ghost and there is in the story, as it is told in the book, a remarkably accurate account of what was presented in the play.

The books tells the story in the following words:

"One of Ireland's best known ghost stories is that of the Coonian Ghost. The story began in 1913 in an isolated farmhouse in the townland of Cornarusland. The house was then occupied by the Murphy family comprising a widow, her son James and five daughters. Within a short period the poltergeist activities in the house had become so pronounced that the Coonian Ghost became national news.

Murphy's house had changed hands several times before they came to it. Some claimed that a pensioner had, at one time, been murdered there. It had passed from Burnsides to Corrigans, to Sherrys and then to Murphys.

According to the story the trouble started before the Murphys resided there. The Sherrys who occupied it for one night only, had the first experience of poltergeist activity in the building. However, they kept quiet about the incident and sold the house six months later to the unsuspecting Murphys.

The Murphys' first encounter with the poltergeist was in the spring of 1913. Mrs Murphy and her daughter, aged 23, were sitting chatting beside the turf fire. The youngest girls, Jeanette, Patricia and Susan were in bed. The eldest, James (25), was on a ceili in a neighbour's house. Suddenly the peaceful atmosphere was shattered by footsteps and tapping on the partition wall. The

*youngest girls screamed with terror but Mrs Murphy and her daughter calmly
began searching for what they thought was a practical joker.*

*Meanwhile, James returned and joined in the search. They searched the
house from top to bottom but could find no explanation for the noise. The
poltergeist activity increased as the weeks went by and neighbours were asked
to come to verify the situation. Several of them also heard noises. In due
course rumours and superstitions became rife and the Murphys found
themselves ostracised by their neighbours. This added to the strain they felt.*

*Two priests, Father Peter Smyth and Father Eugene Coyle, gave the family
good support in the crisis and in doing so witnessed the poltergeist.*

*Father Coyle, a young curate at nearby Maguiresbridge, visited the
farmhouse and told how he stood in the children's bedroom and witnessed the
clothes on the empty bed rising and falling in rhythm to a person's breathing.
He also recalled how pots and pans would suddenly fly from the dresser while
a cold presence filled the room. It was also noticed that when the Murphy girls
were taken from the bedroom to the kitchen the mysterious rappings followed
them but in a more subdued form.*

*Another encounter Father Coyle told of was when he and Father Smyth were
standing side-by-side in a room. It was silent but suddenly there came a
crashing noise from the storey above. Father Coyle stated that it was hard to
describe what followed this outburst. He said it was like a terrific rush of air
between the two of them. It felt as if the ghost resented their very presence in
the house. They heard it and they felt the force of it but not one item of their
clothing had been disturbed. Father Coyle also told of how the ghost would lift
the plates, cups and saucers from the dresser in the kitchen and hurl them to
the floor, and of how the ghost would snatch the bedclothes off the sleeping
children and fling them across the room.*

*Sir Shane Leslie of Glasslough who maintained a life-long interest in the
supernatural and who was the author of a book about Irish Ghosts, has written
of the versatility of the ghost in Murphy's house. 'The Coonian poltergeist was
nothing if not versatile, and it appears to have been gifted with a vast
repertoire. It snored. It emitted noises that appeared to come from far
underground. It took human shape under the sheets of a bed. It pulled the
bedclothes off members of the unfortunate Murphy family. It made a sound like
the kicking of a horse. It hissed and whistled and manifested itself in many
ways. It could even tap out tunes and two of its favourite numbers were 'Boyne
Water' and 'The Soldiers' Song'. As well as being gifted in the variety of its*

performances, the poltergeist apparently was endowed with an intelligence, for it was able to answer correctly questions put to it. This it did by means of tapping.'

The Murphys had enough and decided to emigrate to the United States. They closed up their house with relief. Their passage for the first half of the journey was uneventful but soon they were quickly transported back to reality as they discovered that the poltergeist was still with them. When they reached New York, the ghost haunted them with the same antics. The family were forced to change residence several times but it always followed them. Eventually in 1915 the poltergeist left them for good.

After the Murphys left, the house was sold to William James Montgomery who lived there for five or six years witnessing nothing untoward. He then sold it to Robbie Montgomery. The last occupier was Patrick Warnock. The farm was taken over by the Forestry Service about 35 years ago and the house has been empty since. It is still standing, though it is hardly visible from the road now with the new growth of forestry plantation."

A very similar story from Co. Fermanagh is told in John Richard's book "Deliver us from Evil." It took place in Derrygonnelly and is well documented in the Proceedings of the Society for Psychical Research, Volume 25. It was researched by Sir William Barrett, Professor of Physics at Trinity College, Dublin and a prominent member of the Society. In his report of what was happening in the Derrygonnelly farmhouse, Professor Barrett stated the following: "Knocks were going on everywhere around; all the chairs, the bedstead, the walls and ceiling. Suddenly a large pebble fell in my presence on the bed. No one had moved to dislodge it, even if it had been placed with a purpose. The knocks became still louder like those made by a carpenter's heavy hammer driving nails into flooring. Professor Barrett goes on to say that the people who lived in this house were Methodists. The report continues: "Several neighbours urged them to send for a priest, but they were Methodists, and their class leader advised them to lay an open Bible on the bed. This they did in the name of God, putting a big stone on the top of the volume; but the stone was lifted off by an unseen hand and the Bible placed on top of it. After that 'it', as the father called the unseen cause, moved the Bible out of the room and tore seventeen pages right across."

It was decided by the farmer and his family that a service should be held in the house. One of the investigators, the Rev Maxwell Chase, conducted a short service. Sir William continues his report: "The noises were at first so great we could hardly hear what was read. Then, as the solemn words of prayer were uttered, they subsided. When the Lord's Prayer was joined in by us all, a profound stillness fell on the whole cottage. The farmer rose from his knees with tears streaming from his eyes, gratefully grasped our hands, and we left. I am afraid this does not sound a very scientific account, but it is a veracious one." The report concluded that there were no further disturbances from that night.

Perhaps it was stories like these which had a fascination for me from early days, that led me eventually into a ministry to those who were troubled, and sometimes terrified, by the paranormal. I gain strength from the fact that men of the calibre of a Professor of Physics in Trinity College, Dublin have experienced things which are beyond human explanation. There are more things in heaven and on earth than we can imagine or understand. But nothing is outside the control of him to whom God has given all authority and power. It is the business of the Church to exercise that authority and power in the name of Jesus Christ.

Chapter Two
What about the Devil?

Some years ago the Church of England set up a committee to consider the revision of the Catechism in the old Book of Common Prayer. It needed to be examined with a view to bringing it up-to-date. Its language was archaic and the contents quaint. One of the subjects discussed was the reference to the devil. "They (the godparents) did promise and vow three things in my name: first that I should renounce the devil and all his works." It was argued by some members of the committee that the idea of renouncing the devil and all his works was an anachronism. People did not believe in the devil any more. By all means, let renunciation of sin remain, but do not ask people to say that they renounce the devil.

I have to admit that there was a time in my life, when I might have agreed with removing the devil from the official teaching of the Church. The probability is, that I would have voted against the majority decision to keep the devil in the formularies of the Church. Like those who may choose to read this book, I have been brought up with a scientific world view. I have never found it easy to grasp the concept of a being whom we call Satan, Beelzebub or the Devil whose purpose and aim is to lead people away from God into sin and rebellion. Just as difficult for me has been the clear teaching of the New Testament which tells us that under this being, there is an army of lesser beings called demons, whose job is to control, influence or destroy lives.

Obviously I'm not the only one who has experienced these difficulties at one time or another. I seem to remember imbibing the idea during my training for the Ministry, that the concept of a personalised devil sprang from primitive peoples who tend to personalise the cause of every inexplicable thing that happens to them. When evil strikes the cause is personalised and it becomes the work of the devil. I have no doubt that there are men in Christian Ministry, including Bishops, who hold that view. I cannot criticise them or impute blame for that was my own vague notion for some years after my ordination. It is amazing that we can ask the question in the Baptism Service: "Do you renounce the devil and all his works?", having little or no conviction that he really does exist.

How then have I come to believe with full conviction that the devil does exist? How have I come to believe that demons can impinge on, and influence the life of, people today? It is not only because it is the plain teaching of scripture but also because of what I have observed and experienced in life. Like most of my strongly held convictions, it has come in part from experience. Seeing is believing. Experience teaches a fool. In the early seventies I met someone who relieved me of all my doubts.

She was a young woman, probably still in her twenties. When I met her she was in a Belfast hospital where I was a chaplain. In the course of talking with her and ministering to her as a hospital chaplain, she came to a decision to repent of her sins and put her trust in Jesus Christ. Everything went well for a time. She was in Church every Sunday and sat in the front pew. She joined a group that met in the Rectory for fellowship and prayer every week.

The first lapse came one evening when I received a call from the police that Alice (not her real name) was in the police station and very drunk. It was well after midnight. I dressed and went to pick her up. Her first words to me when I arrived at the station were, "I thought that God was supposed to be looking after me."

I brought her back to the Rectory and we put her to bed. She was very drunk. Things began to go wrong from that evening. She became a burden and a source of anxiety. One evening, I received a call from a church member with whom Alice was staying for a few days. "Will you come and talk with Alice? She is very difficult and I can do nothing with her." I went immediately and found things just as I had been told. Alice was being very difficult, argumentative, nasty, unreasonable and truculent. I talked with her for a while trying to get her to be reasonable and co-operative. I had never seen this side of her before. She was scowling and ugly. Then I noticed something very strange in her ranting. She seemed to be talking about someone else and not herself. She was using the words "she" and "her." What was she talking about? I was confused. Suddenly I saw what was happening. She was talking about herself in the third person. She was not using "I" and "me". She was using "she" and "her." It was someone else that was doing the talking. It was someone else or something else that was arguing with me about her. When I grasped the situation, my adrenaline began to flow. It was my turn to get aggressive. I felt angry. I was confronting evil.

I had read about this kind of thing and now I had come face to face with it. I knew too that the Lord had given authority to his Church to cast out demons. So I confronted the demon and commanded it to leave. I cannot remember how long the battle continued while the lady of the house looked on in amazement and prayed. Probably less than five minutes. The demon continued to argue, "You can't get rid of me little man. You're making a fool of yourself. She belongs to me. I knew her before you knew her." My commands in the name of Jesus and in the power of the Spirit were just as strong and as fierce as what was being hurled back at me. Suddenly there was a loud scream and Alice fell to the ground and lay there in silence for a couple of minutes. It was like a repeat of what happened in Capernaum "The evil spirit shook the man violently and came out of him with a shriek." (Mark 1.26).

Alice recovered consciousness and sat up looking very puzzled. "How did I get here on the floor? What happened?" Then she addressed me, "How long have you been here?" She was now her usual self and speaking normally. Obviously there had been no communication between her and me since I arrived. She was shut out and the demon had taken over. Psychiatrists who cannot accept the possibility that demons are real will have another explanation for Alice's behaviour but I am firmly convinced that what I saw and heard was a demonstration of demonic power and activity.

If that experience was my only encounter with personalised evil in Alice, I might be able to put it down as a one-off event with a scientific explanation. However, there is more to the story than that. I wish I could write that from that day on everything was well with Alice. The truth is, it was not. This was only the beginning of sorrows. Enquiries revealed that Alice had been formally initiated into a satanic group when she was younger. She had gone through a ceremony in which vows were made to obey and serve Satan. She was given a satanic name and other disgusting events took place which I will not attempt to describe. These things were unearthed in a number of conversations over a period of weeks.

Finally, it was decided that a major exorcism was necessary. A small team that included a doctor and myself was assembled and an exorcism was attempted. It was obvious from the start that Alice was not totally in favour, but reluctantly, she agreed. I will not try to describe in detail all that happened. We made progress at first, casting out several demons that came to the surface, mocking and jeering. In the end, there came a point when Alice refused to co-operate with us any further. It was then we realised that further progress was not going to be made. She refused to disclose her satanic name or the name of the group into which she had been initiated. In the end the most curious and grotesque thing of all happened. Alice walked away and stood in a corner of the room with her back to us. We heard her speaking in a low voice as if she were praying. She was praying, but not to God. We heard her say: "They're trying to take me away from you but they will not succeed. I'm going to stay with you." That settled the matter for us and it showed me something important about exorcism. You will not be successful if the person you are trying to help fights against you. That seems to give demons the legal right to be there and the power to resist.

So Alice passed out of our influence. Occasionally I would see her at a distance plying her illicit trade, the sorry sight of a young woman grown old before her time and bearing the marks of a life destroyed by demonic power. She died in her early forties and I can still recall the melancholy horror and sadness I felt when I learned of her death in a doorway in the red light area of Belfast.

Having witnessed that awful scene, I cannot say other than that demons exist. I stand wholeheartedly alongside that great Irishman C S Lewis when he wrote these words in his Screwtape Letters:

"There are two equal and opposite errors into which our race can fall about the devils. One is to disbelieve in their existence. The other is to believe and to feel an excessive and unhealthy interest in them. They themselves are equally pleased by both errors and hail a materialist or a magician with the same delight."

In describing how I came to believe in the reality of demonic power it is not my intention to attribute all the evil in the world to the devil and his cohorts. Let's not give him more credit than he deserves. We need to recall what we were taught in Sunday School, that temptation and consequently evil, come from three sources: the world (the foe around us), the flesh (the foe within) and the devil (the foe beneath). It is still a good idea to consider all three possibilities when looking for the source of the evil that afflicts us.

Chapter Three

The Occult

During my fifty years in the ordained ministry of the Church of Ireland, I have prepared many adults and children for their confirmation. At no time did I find it necessary to teach about the occult and to warn against its inherent dangers. Perhaps that was due to a lack of thought or imagination on my part. Today some of those who prepare young people for confirmation touch on many issues that did not arise in days gone by, such as drugs, alcohol, sexual morality and the occult.

It is significant that today's young people know what is meant by the word "occult." The question: "Have you ever been involved with the occult?" does not need to be explained. If I had been asked that question at sixteen years of age when I was confirmed, I would have had no idea of what was being asked. The word occult was not in my vocabulary. It is in many young people's vocabulary today. That shows an interest in, and perhaps an involvement with, occult practice. On occasions I have been asked to come and address young people on the subject of the occult.

Francis McNutt writes in his book "Deliverance from Evil Spirits"

> "The occult (the word comes from the Latin for 'hidden' or 'secret') represents the spiritual realm where people seek either knowledge or power from any source other than God, when the kind of knowledge or power sought can come only from God. When we seek such power or knowledge, we are opening ourselves, even when we do not realise what we are doing, to the realm of evil spirits. The vast majority of people who get involved in the occult do not realise they are doing anything wrong."

The occultist searches for truth in the hidden areas of life, especially in contact with what so-called spiritualists describe as "the other side." The promise held out by the occult to its adherents is that of passing beyond the limits of man's normal knowledge and experience.

The common and better-known occult practices are usually approached in a light-hearted manner and are considered by some as a "bit of fun" and "good for a laugh." Such practices are fortune telling by various means, such as crystal gazing, palm-reading and the use of tarot cards; ouija, which some regard as a game; attempting to contact the dead through a medium or at a seance; levitation which means the raising of a body by supernatural means. These practices which are well known amongst schoolchildren and students are practised by people today, perhaps in greater numbers than we think. They are dangerous and forbidden in Holy Scripture.

> "Let no one be found among you ... who practises divination or sorcery, interprets omens, engages in witchcraft, or casts spells or who is a medium or a spiritist or who consults the dead. Anyone who does these things is detestable to the Lord..." (Deuteronomy 18.10)

> "I will set my face against the person who turns to mediums and spiritists to prostitute himself by following them..." (Leviticus 20.6)

> "Do not turn to mediums or seek out spirits, for you will be defiled by them." (Leviticus 19.31)

> "A number who had practised sorcery brought their scrolls together and burned them publicly. When they calculated the value of the scrolls, the total came to 50,000 drachmas" (A footnote tells us that one drachma equals a day's wages.) These were the scrolls of those who had been converted to Christ and had forsaken their former occult ways. (Acts 19.19)

> "The Spirit clearly says that in later times some will abandon the faith and follow deceiving spirits and things taught by demons." (1 Timothy 4.1)

There are so many varieties of occult practice that it is useful to think of them under four general headings.

1 – Ouija

This game, as some would call it, is played out on a smooth board with the letters of the alphabet arranged in a circle. The board is placed on a table and an upturned glass is placed in the middle of the circle. A form of meditation or concentration is then employed by a small group gathered round the board. The fingers of each person are placed on the glass and questions are asked, sometimes using the preface "spirit of the glass." The questions are answered as the upturned glass begins to move from one letter to another, spelling out answers.

It is easy to see how fascinating this "game" could be to children or adults.

In some cases it has become addictive with dire results. It seems at first sight to be harmless and therein lies the danger.

Once the question is asked: "Where do the answers come from?", the possibility of deadly defilement from evil sources becomes apparent. Those around the table may be in touch with dark forces from another realm. Many stories from well-known writers have been told illustrating the dangers of ouija. (See Anne's story, Part 1, chapter 4   ).

2 – Spiritism

I am using the word spiritism deliberately. The person who calls himself a spiritualist prefers to speak of himself as a "sensitive at a spiritualist church, contacting those on the other side." It sounds better than mediums in spiritist groups practising what the Bible calls necromancy. It means the same thing, (Deuteronomy (18.11 A.V.). Spiritism is an attempt to be in touch with spirits.

The problem for those who attend spiritist groups or gatherings is that they cannot be sure of the kind of spirit with which they are dealing. It may be a demonic or evil spirit. If God has forbidden this practice as I have shown he has, it is a nonsense to suggest that the messages from the other side are from the spirits of loved ones. Would God allow what he has described as detestable to take place? Would we want our loved ones who are at rest, to be involved in what is described in scripture as a defilement? Paul refers to "deceiving spirits". That is the nature of demons. Their purpose is to deceive and lie and promote what is false. What an opportunity they have when the unwary, unsuspecting, impressionable and gullible come to a spiritist gathering, perhaps moved by sorrow, curiosity, loneliness or fear. They are opening themselves to receive what the Lord has forbidden.

Sometimes spiritist activity takes place in a Spiritualist Church during a Service. It takes on an atmosphere of normality and respectability. Hymns are sung, prayers are said, scriptures are read and a sermon is preached. A medium is employed to communicate messages from the other side as the place of the departed is called.

One way that that is done and which I have witnessed, is that the medium goes into a trance. I recall heavy breathing while that was taking place. The lights were turned off and an infra-red light was directed on the medium's face. His body was then taken over in turn by his three "guides" and they began to speak their messages from the so called other side. One voice was Scottish, and one said to be Chinese spoke in broken English. I cannot recall the third.

I came away very unimpressed in those days by the whole procedure. As I look back to that event of nearly forty years ago, I am horrified at what was taking place before my eyes. A man was deliberately opening himself to the entry of spirits and giving them the use of his body to speak to that group of people. They were not departed spirits but deceiving spirits with false messages. To be in their presence and pay heed to what is said is not only foolishness. It is foolhardiness and should be shunned.

After the two world wars of the twentieth century, there was an increase of interest in spiritism. That is not surprising in a situation where so many people had lost loved ones and longed to know their condition. Had they survived death? Were they happy and content? What was life like for them in their new environment? Did they remember their loved ones still on earth? The desire to find answers to these questions was almost overwhelming for some poor, grief-stricken relatives and they succumbed to the temptation to use whatever means were available to them, to ease their grief and find comfort. That is perfectly understandable and one must show sympathy with the bereaved. It is unrealistic to declare that all those who seek the help of a medium will be permanently damaged. No one can or should say that. However, let everyone who is tempted to use a medium realise that to do so incurs serious risks. I am bound by scripture and in good conscience to advise as strongly as I can against it.

There are certain important things that must be taken into consideration.

(a) This is forbidden territory. King Saul's contact with the witch of Endor ended in disaster (1 Samuel 28.4-19 and 31.1-4).

(b) There is not any certainty, nor can there be, that those who attend spiritist groups are in touch with departed loved ones. The awful possibility is that they are in touch with deceiving spirits who can impersonate the departed.

(c) By seeking to make contact with the departed we are leaving ourselves open to the possibility of coming under the influence of powerful and evil entities. Canon Michael Harper writes: "We have found that the vast majority of those who need exorcism have been involved in spiritism."

3 – Witchcraft

A witch may be defined as a woman (a male witch is called a wizard), who is supposed to have dealings with the devil or evil spirits and by their cooperation is able to perform supernatural acts. They operate in covens or individually. They practise magic - black and white. In black magic they attempt to produce evil results through such methods as curses, spells, destruction of models of the enemy and alliance with evil spirits. In white magic they try to undo curses and spells and to use occult forces for their good and the good of others. The New Bible Dictionary (I.V.F.) states the following:

> "There is no doubt that magic and sorcery are not always mere superstition but have reality behind them. They must be resisted and overcome through the power of God in the name of Jesus Christ."

Does witchcraft exist today? I have no evidence based on personal experience so I must rely on what I have learnt from others. John Richard, a clergyman of the Church of England, took a year's sabbatical to write his book "Deliver us from Evil", published in 1974. His book is one of the most detailed and carefully documented books on the paranormal. He writes as follows about witchcraft: "Witchcraft is wide-spread. The German Medical Information Service states that 10,000 people are engaged in witchcraft in Germany." In a BBC television programme "The power of the Witch", the estimate for Britain was three times as many! I cannot claim to have any personal knowledge of covens or witches in this community. Covens are by their very nature hidden and secret but it is reasonable to suppose that if they exist in Germany and Great Britain they exist in Ireland too.

Witches have openly declared themselves on "TV chat shows" and have presented themselves as people of ordinary appearance, often intelligent, articulate and convincing. Therein lies the danger! The old hag with a hooked nose and black cone-shaped hat was a figure of fun and deceived nobody. The present day model with blue eyes and blonde hair is more attractive and could conceivably draw into a coven those who are searching for more power in life. People should be warned that things are not what they appear to be.

4 – Satanism

We are now getting into an extremely dangerous area. There is a parallel here with entry to the drug scene. The soft drugs come first. Marijuana may be the way it all begins. Perhaps it does not seem very serious but it is often the way in. Then follow the more addictive drugs leading eventually to cocaine and heroin and enslavement. That is how it is with getting involved with the occult. It begins in a small way, moves on to serious experimentation and ends with the loss of freedom and self-respect.

Satanists are those who have made a deliberate act of allegiance to Satan and a corresponding renunciation of Jesus Christ and the Church. They commit themselves to a way of life that is not only un-Christian but totally anti-Christian. In that way it is a more serious evil than witchcraft. Witchcraft may declare itself to be un-Christian in its words and deeds, but it is not deliberately anti-Christian. Satanism is in total opposition to everything that is good. It is intrinsically, totally and absolutely evil.

To write on this subject as I have tried to do has not been easy. There is a dark, dirty and devilish stench about it. I can well understand the words of Douglas Hunt in his book "Exploring the Occult" :

"No warning against any participation in real or alleged Black Magic can be strong enough. Have nothing to do with it, do not enquire into it and shun like the plague anyone you know involved in it....it is dirty, childish and bestial. It can lead to nothing but a contemptible depravity"

When Jesus taught His disciples to pray He was careful to add this petition: "Deliver us from evil." It is more accurately translated: "Deliver us from the evil one." That petition was not an afterthought. The Lord's Prayer includes the elements of all true Christian prayer. As such, it covers man's need of deliverance from a cunning, lying and relentless enemy. He is a foolish man who ignores that need.

An activity that is associated with witches and Satanists is cursing, sometimes called ill-wishing or death-wishing. Most people in this country would describe the practice of cursing as mediaeval superstition. There is no doubt that the idea of cursing is found in Holy Scripture and is forbidden for God's people. Jesus said: "Bless those who curse you, pray for those who ill-treat you". (Luke 6.28). Paul writes: "Bless those who persecute you. Bless and do not curse". (Romans 12.14). James writes: "Out of the same mouth come praise and cursing. My brothers this should not be". (James 3.10). Whether this means deliberately putting a curse on someone is open to question and requires serious thought. It should not be dismissed lightly.

John Richard in "Deliver us from Evil" states the following:

"The problem of all ill-wishing or cursing is not a problem for many because they simply do not believe it. Those who do believe in the reality of it, will either themselves have been on the receiving end of such things, or have had the pastoral care of someone so affected. Even if the mechanics of it can be described as auto-suggestion, the symptoms are as real as any other psychosomatic disorder and present something to be healed whatever our personal views about the ultimate causes. The Christian Minister is not committed to any particular theory of curses, but he is committed to bringing the resources of the healing church, the healing Christ, to the situation".

A few years ago I ministered to a young woman who believed she was cursed. Georgia (not her real name) came from Nigeria. She was born of rich parents and was very intelligent. She had two university degrees, one in America and one in this country. Her father had been married twice. Her brother and she were children of the second marriage. The first wife was deeply involved with occult practices and, because of her prowess in such matters, was "worshipped" during her life-time and after her death. Georgia's own mother brought her brother and herself to a witch-doctor when they were very young for his help. (My notes do not record the reason for this visitation.) They bear the mark of the witch doctor on their bodies to this day.

It was Georgia's unshakeable conviction that a curse had been put on both of them. When Georgia came to this country she was married to a psychiatrist and had three children. Her husband divorced her and took the children with him, leaving her penniless. She had not seen or heard from them for years and had no idea where they were.

When I visited her in a flat near the Royal Victoria Hospital, she was living with the bare minimum of necessities for life. She was highly qualified in the medical field and had applied for dozens of jobs but was always unsuccessful. After every application that she made, she had a dream. In her dream a black man came to her, taunting her and saying that she would never get a job for he had cursed her. Her brother was still in Nigeria and was suffering a similar fate. He who had been born with a rich father had resorted to begging in his own country.

Georgia came to a service of the Divine Healing Ministries in St Anne's Cathedral, desperately looking for help. She was passed on to me. At that time I had no personal experience of ministering to someone who believed herself to be cursed. The only thing that I knew for certain was that to Jesus belonged all authority and power.

My wife and I befriended her, bringing her home and to church on Sunday evenings. She attended a Methodist church on Sunday mornings. Georgia was determined to be free of the curse that she believed had been laid upon her.

Someone at the Christian Renewal Centre in Rostrevor gave her a book by Derek Prince called "Blessing or Curse: You can choose". It was a closely reasoned book and of some length. She studied it in detail, reading every sentence and making careful notes. Eventually she decided what to do. She produced an Order of Service for revoking every curse against her and asked me as a Priest of the Church of Ireland to perform the Service. I was glad and honoured to do so. The service was carefully written out in considerable detail. It came to seven pages which I have kept in my possession. Every possible curse was revoked in the name of Jesus and my job as a priest was to exercise the authority he has given to his Church.

About a fortnight after the service I had a letter from Georgia. She was leaving Belfast. She had just been given a job in a large Birmingham hospital in the field of medical research. The years of searching in vain for employment were over. She was overjoyed. Some people may have serious doubts about this sequel to a Service of Deliverance. How did it happen? Was it a coincidence? Had the Service of Revoking Curses anything to do with it? Who can be sure? Georgia had no doubts. She gave God the glory.

Chapter Four

The Destructive Power of Ouija

A survey carried out some years ago revealed that out of 80,000 children questioned, 80% had been involved in some way with ouija sessions or playground seances. Naturally, people will ask questions about what lies behind ouija activity. Where do the answers of the "spirit of the glass" come from? Has it something to do with the collective sub-conscious of the partakers? Is it a deliberate fraud? Is it a little bit of trickery by someone in the circle? Those who have been frightened and terrified of what has happened at a ouija session, will not see it that way. Those whose lives have been blighted for years as a result of playing with a ouija board, will not be impressed by the claim that it's only a harmless game.

I have permission to share with you the story of a lady whose life was tormented for fifteen years as a result of two sessions of playing the ouija in her home.

Anne's Story

My story begins in November 1964. I was a young mother of two boys and a girl. My husband was a banquet manager in a leading hotel in Belfast. His work meant that he was often away from home for long periods and did a lot of night work, so our times together and with the children were precious. I made sure that I was always available for the children when they came home from school.

One day my elder boy who was fifteen years of age came home very excited. He had discovered a new game at school and it worked like magic, answering all the questions that were asked of it. It knew about the future, where someone would work, whom he would marry, where he would live, what kind of work he would do. All that was necessary was a circle of the letters of the alphabet on the table, the words 'yes' and 'no' in the circle and an upturned drinking glass in the middle. I had lived in Co. Tyrone for a time and had seen this done, so I recognised this game.

The children coaxed me to set it up for them on the dining room table. We began with the question: "Is anyone there?" To our amazement, the glass moved round the 'yes' several times.

We went on to ask: "Who are you?" Answers came back telling us that he was a sea man who had been killed on the H.M.S. Victory. The answers were always in old English using "thou" and "hast". We stopped it because I was getting a little concerned.

Next afternoon the weather was bad so my son said, "Let's do it again and see what we get this time." So, we set it up and asked, "Is anyone there?" After "yes", I asked, "Who are you?" Answer: Pierre Dubois. Are you living or dead? Answer: Dead. Where did you die? Answer: In the French Revolution. After further questioning, we were given the date of his death, and where he lived in France.

Things began to change at this stage. We did not need to ask questions any more. It was as if the glass was alive. It began to address me. "Anne, I would like to stay here with you. I am tired wandering and need rest. I was with relations in South Africa but was not wanted there". Then it said, "Anne, go into the kitchen and shut the window. The rain is getting in." I went to the kitchen and the window had blown open and the floor was wet.

At that point, my husband came home and looked into the living-room and enquired what we were doing. I told him that we were playing a game to pass the time. When he saw what it was, he said it was a foolish thing to do and went to bed to get some rest, before going back to work late in the evening. The glass began to move immediately without any questions being asked. "Robert does not believe in me, but I will come to him tonight as a ghost." "Oh, please don't do that. Go away." I was getting frightened. "No more of this children" I said. "It isn't fun any more." With that, I threw all the bits and pieces into the fire and tried to forget all about it.

I was still awake after midnight when my husband returned home. "I hope you stopped playing that silly game." he said. I joked about it, "I wouldn't like to be you. It said it was going to come to you tonight as a ghost." We laughed and soon Robert was asleep. I lay awake. There was an awful coldness that came over the room. I saw the bedroom door opening very slowly and something terribly heavy lay on top of me. I was pinned to the bed and I heard heavy breathing. My body stiffened and I went into a spasm. I was paralysed from head to toe. I tried to call out to my husband but words would not come. I tried to raise my hand to touch him but my arm would not move. How long I lay like this I do not know. I thought I was dying. Dawn was beginning to break when the weight began to lift. Slowly, I began to move my fingers, hands and arms. My heart was pounding. At last I was able to waken my husband. I could hardly speak to tell him what had happened. I felt very ill. My husband had to get up and get the children off to school. I did not tell my family anything of what had happened because I did not want to frighten them.

On the next night I was alone going to bed because my husband was not able to be home till morning. I put my Bible under my pillow and another beside my bed. I got down on my knees to ask God's forgiveness and help. The same things happened as on the previous night. I was so upset, I went to visit my doctor. He told me that I looked dreadful and was in a state of shock. I told him what had happened. He said that I could probably be a medium but I assured him I did not want to be that. He prescribed medicine to calm me down and said that I should ask for God's help.

My home was never the same after that. I felt uncomfortable, especially when I was alone. I began singing French songs and the French National Anthem although I had never learnt French. My husband was away at nights a lot and I was terrified of going to bed. I sat up very late. I confided in a few friends but kept my fears to myself, in case I would be misunderstood.

Things seemed to calm down somewhat after a time. Then things changed. When lying in bed, my pillow would be beaten quite hard, so hard that my head bounced. This would happen only when I was alone. The lights would flicker and the water-taps would be turned on, when nobody was near them. My friends began to notice the creaking of the floorboards upstairs. My little daughter (12) and tiny son (5) began to tell me about mice in their bedroom.

As the months and years went by, my family seemed to be not too disturbed but gradually things got worse for me. I did not talk about it in case people would think I was mad. Night was the worst time for me, for I knew that someone was waiting for me to retire. Strange things were still happening. When I was sound asleep all my bed clothes would be whisked off the bed and laid out on the floor at the bottom of the bed in one sweep. I got so used to this that I would wake up, replace the bedclothes and go to sleep again. Worse was to come.

As I was alone in the house for long periods, I decided to look for a job and found one as a shop assistant. This took me away from the house for most of the day. When I returned each evening, I had this strong feeling that something or someone was waiting for me. Things began to get really bad again, indeed much worse. I would waken up in the middle of the night by this dreadful weight, almost squeezing the breath out of me. I would cry out "Dear God, help me!" and it would ease off for a time. When I was so tired that I could not keep my eyes open, it would happen again.

I had a little Roman Catholic friend at work in whom I confided, but not telling her everything. She said that she had heard of that kind of thing and told me to say: "In the name of Jesus Christ get out of my life." I was determined to try. As usual I waited that night as long as possible before going to bed. I read until my eyes closed. That is when things would normally begin to happen. This time there was a new development. I began to hear a "zooming" noise getting nearer and nearer to my bed and then the awful weight on top of me. I felt it was trying to kill me so that I could join him wherever he was. I cried out again, "Dear God, don't let me die. I don't want to see his face." I pushed with all my strength against this invisible thing and sat up and said, "In the name of Jesus Christ, get out of my life!" A loud voice that seemed to be coming from the ceiling said back to me, "Be quiet and go to sleep." Immediately I went to sleep. Next day, when I thought about that, it frightened me even more for this thing seemed to have power over me. These strange disturbances would continue for a week and then cease for a while. It went on for years and I could do nothing but accept it. At times I was exhausted for lack of sleep.

My sister told a few of her friends about the trouble I was having. One of the girls was a good committed Christian girl and sent me a lovely gold framed picture. It reads: "Christ is the head of this house, the unseen guest at every meal, the silent listener to every conversation." She hoped I would hang it up in my bedroom to see if it would help. I did that. That night, I went to bed feeling I had some protection and was soon fast asleep. I was wakened up at 2.00 am by an awful noise. First, I thought it was a dog barking. It seemed to fill the room. Then I realised it was a horrible, mocking laugh. I put the bedclothes over my head and I don't think I got any more sleep that night.

I call to mind one year when I went on holiday and left my eldest son Ivan in charge of the house. I hadn't told him anything of what I was suffering. When I got home he said to me, "There is no way I would stay in this house alone again. I wakened up several times with something beating my pillow and I felt there was something creepy about the landing. It was always cold, no matter how high I turned up the heat." I decided that he was now old enough to hear my story, so I told him of some of the things that had happened to me without going into the sordid details. Having told him, I was now worried for him.

After that holiday in 1978 and a visit to my daughter in Dublin, I returned refreshed. It was marvellous for me to get sound, undisturbed sleep. However, when I got home things began to happen again with a vengeance. I wakened from sleep to find myself struggling with an invisible creature. I could feel clamp-like hands around my throat, forcing my head into the pillow. I fought with all the strength I had and called for God to help me. With that, the weight eased. Next day, I was very distressed and told my husband, sister and brother-in-law what had happened.

My husband worked at night which meant I slept alone. It was decided that I should sleep in a small room downstairs, so a bed was put there for me. While in bed, I kept the radio playing soft music and I read until sleep overcame me. The light was kept on. I had just closed my eyes when the zooming noise started getting nearer and nearer and then the awful weight again. I forced myself straight up and shouted the words I had repeated on previous occasions. Slowly, it eased away. I kept the Bible on my chest the rest of the night.

Next day, I was feeling awful. My health was beginning to suffer. I could not go on. I must do something. I must get help. I told my story to a girl called Sheila. She was appalled that I had suffered so much and for so long. It was fifteen years. Sheila asked me if I would allow her to tell my problem to another girl called Margaret who might be able to help me. I was glad to receive any help I could get.

She arranged for me to go to St Mary Magdalene Church, Donegall Pass, Belfast that very night to meet the Rector, the Revd. W H Lendrum. Margaret came with me. He put me at ease right away for I was very nervous. He listened sympathetically to my story and arranged to visit my house when it suited me. I am ashamed to say that I delayed his visit a few days because I was having some work done in my house and the place was untidy. Strangely, he warned me that things might get worse now that plans were being laid to get rid of this thing, and that is exactly what happened.

The house was quiet after my son left and I began to clean up the dirt left by the workmen. There was a dreadful atmosphere that I cannot describe. I had a new vacuum cleaner which gave out the most odd sound, like a person groaning. It frightened me, so I switched it off and decided to read. That proved impossible. Should I call my Managing Director, Mr Ruddock, who was a good Christian man? I decided not for he might think I was being silly. So I rang my son Ivan who had gone to a friend's house. I didn't need to say anything. He knew by the sound of my voice that I was frightened so he came home at once. When he arrived, his face was ashen. He had had a horrific ride home. The car seemed to be driving itself and he was nearly involved in an accident. I was in tears and so glad of his company. Eventually we retired to bed. There was still this awful atmosphere. I lay there, wondering what would come next. I felt myself going very cold and shivering and then, just as quickly going warm again. This continued most of the night. I was glad to see daybreak and got up to make Ivan and myself a cup of tea. After enquiring how I was, he told me he had an awful night going hot and cold all night, just as I had done.

I went into work that morning and told Margaret I could not wait any longer. I would ask Mr Lendrum to come as soon as possible. When I called him, he said he was expecting a call and would come that very evening. He came with his good friend Alex Weir. In their presence I renounced all my involvement with ouija and asked for God's forgiveness. I was assured of God's love for me and His total forgiveness.

A service of Holy Communion was held and the spirit who had tormented me for fifteen years was commanded in the name of Jesus Christ to leave, to go to its own place and never to return. Then the Rector went to every room and part of the house and said a prayer asking God to bless it and to send angels to protect it from all evil.

The effect was immediate. A peace descended on the house. The dark cloud lifted. I had my home and my life back again. To this servant of God and his friend, I shall be eternally grateful. To God be all the glory.

Author's Comment

The exorcism took place on 3 July 1980. I kept in touch with Anne after that and am still in touch with her occasionally. She has enjoyed peace and contentment in her home ever since. Her husband died a few years ago and her family have grown up and have homes of their own, so she lives alone. It would be hard to meet a more pleasant and cheerful lady in spite of a decline in her health. She suffers from chronic asthma, which is kept under control with drugs prescribed by her doctor. Anne has always been glad to testify to what the Lord did for her, when He delivered her from such a great evil that was destroying her life. She told her story in "Sunday Sequence", Radio Ulster, BBC, when she was interviewed by the Revd. Trevor Williams.

Chapter Five
Poltergeist Activity

Poltergeist activity is well-known to those who have studied the paranormal. There are many examples that have come down to us across the centuries and they have not been confined to the superstitious or irreligious. One of the better-known cases is called the Epworth Poltergeist, so called because it took place in Epworth Rectory, the home of the Rev. Samuel Wesley, father of John Wesley. It demonstrated all the usual phenomena associated with a poltergeist.

The word poltergeist means a noisy ghost and the ghost in Epworth Rectory seems to have been all that! The knockings and bangings were described "as if all the bottles under the stairs had been dashed to a thousand pieces." The story is well documented in letters written by the Rector and his wife and two daughters. Samuel Wesley and another clergyman called Hoole gave personal accounts of what they experienced and these were verified by their manservant and John Wesley himself. The Wesley family's correspondence containing the relevant passages about the Epworth Polgergeist may be found in the Encyclopaedia of Witchcraft and Demonology (Robbins-Spring Books).

There are certain definite characteristics or traits which suggest the presence and activity of a poltergeist. Reference has already been made to noise but there are other things as well which are observable and upsetting to those who witness them or their effects. Objects are moved from one place to another and whilst the actual movement may not always be observed, there have been severe cases, well documented, when objects have been seen moving and in mid-air. Such movements have not always followed a straight course. Their trajectory will not follow the natural laws but may move in an elliptical or circular course and go round corners.

Another peculiar feature of the poltergeist is that electrical equipment will be activated, electric lights will be turned on and off, and electric doorbells will ring when switches or push-buttons are not touched by human hand. It is reported in a paper produced by the Christian Exorcism Study Group set up by a former Bishop of Exeter, that there have been cases " where the phenomena include interference with electrical apparatus causing it to function independently of its normal power supply."

There has been scientific investigation into poltergeist activity. The main conclusions of the Bishop of Exeter Study Group are as follows:

1. The poltergeist is not a spirit, ghost or demon. It is a force or source of energy called telekinesis (sometimes psychokinesis) which is defined as "the influence of mind on external objects or processes without the mediation of known physical energies or forces."

2. The poltergeist has a human epi-centre or "owner" who unconsciously supplies the energy or force which manifests itself in the phenomena that we call poltergeist activity.

3. The "owner" of the poltergeist, who remains unaware of his or her connection with the poltergeist, is usually a young person who is going through some severe form of mental or emotional trauma. Typical examples are young girls approaching puberty, boys of a sensitive disposition who may be under pressure to pass an important examination, a highly-strung business man who is under pressure at work or at home. These are examples from real cases.

4. Poltergeist activity lasts on average about six weeks to three months but there have been cases known to last up to six months. The activity starts quietly, builds up to a climax and then gradually fades away.

5. Whilst a poltergeist in a home is a frightening experience, it is normally harmless although random, chaotic and mischievous in its activities.

My favourite poltergeist story is about what happened in a false teeth factory in England. The manager's wife was a strong no-nonsense type of lady and her husband was a timid man who was rather too easy going in her eyes with his employees. As a result he was under a considerable strain at home and at work. Curious and mysterious happenings began to take place at the factory. Objects went missing and were being found in strange and inappropriate places. It seemed there was a practical joker in the place and the manager's wife came down to sort things out and stop this nonsense. She would not put up with this kind of thing. While she was there lecturing and threatening the employees, a set of false teeth went missing. She set her handbag down very purposefully on a chair and said she would "get to the bottom of this." She searched every man in the place, every cupboard, shelf and drawer but the teeth could not be found. Totally frustrated she was forced to give up the search and decided to go home. She reached for her handbag to take out her car keys - and a set of false teeth were grinning up at her from her handbag! The poltergeist was doing its job.

Although it is generally agreed that the poltergeist is not a spirit, ghost or demon, it does seem from its actions to have personality as indicated in the above true story. Many other examples could be given to illustrate that. Although a poltergeist's activity seems to be purposeless and puerile, making it a disturbance and a nuisance, some explanation of its activities suggesting a mind at work, cannot be ruled out.

There are two theories that are rather vague and speculative. One is that the "owner" or epi-centre, who unconsciously supplies the energy behind the activity, also unconsciously supplies the motive. How that can be proved or explained is not clear. We are dealing with an inexact science. Psychiatrists may attempt an answer but theologians will be content to regard these things as one of the mysteries of God's creation.

The other theory put forward is that some other entity may be able to latch on to the pyschic energy released by the very disturbed individual in the family. That would mean that what goes on in poltergeist activity is caused, but not motivated or directed, by the "owner", the one who supplies the energy. Who or what this motivating or directing entity may be is not stated. The truth is, that while we know something about poltergeist activity and what lies behind it, there is much more that we do not know. It should be noted that poltergeist activity is not common. In nearly thirty years I have experienced only three cases.

The most fully documented case, that I have experienced, was near Randalstown, Co Antrim. Someone asked me to investigate a haunt, not poltergeist activity. I travelled to see the place with my wife and two other friends. The house was occupied by Michael and his partner Anne and two daughters, Rosemary aged 15 and Susan aged 4 (not their real names). The children were the off-spring of former marriages. Rosemary was Michael's child and Susan was Anne's. The haunt was described to us in some detail.

Michael and Anne had moved into the house with the two children a few months earlier. It was an old farmhouse, situated in a long country lane with the usual farmhouse yard and various store places outside. From time to time the figure of a woman in a long skirt and a man's jacket was seen both inside and outside the house. Neighbours too were aware of the apparition. The figure was usually seen in the kitchen or walking about the farmyard. Occasionally it would appear at the window when the dog would bark ferociously but refuse to go outside. On several occasions a woman could be heard singing upstairs and having a conversation with Susan (4) who had been put to bed. At first Susan complained about "the lady" but seemed to get used to her.

One of Michael's sons (a teenager) came to visit and stay for the night. He slept in the living-room with the moon shining through the window. In the middle of the night he wakened to see a figure pass through the room. Not knowing anything about what was going on in the house, he assumed it was Anne and went to sleep. The next day he enquired why Anne was up during the night. She had not been up!

This is a brief outline of what we heard in considerable detail. It sounds unreal in cold print, but sitting down with the family and hearing the story from their own lips, it was obvious to us that something must be done. We had come to help. Our diagnosis was that this was a clear case of an earth-bound spirit - a spirit that had got "stuck" - and needed to be helped on to the next stage of its journey. I decided to "release" this spirit by celebrating a service of the Holy Communion in the house. (I will give other examples in Part 2 Chapter 6 and describe how I deal with haunts and similar phenomena.) It is sufficient at this point to say that the apparition was not seen again.

Sometimes one form of paranormal activity triggers another. In this case the haunt followed by an "exorcism" successfully carried out, triggered extensive and severe poltergeist activity so I returned to the scene with my companions some days later. The woman with the long skirt, man's jacket and boots was no longer seen. We listened now to a different story describing strange events, indeed.

I will begin with what we were shown. Anne had taken Susan (5) to school that day. She was absent from the house about twenty minutes. When she returned, she found that Susan's bed had been taken out of her bedroom and placed on the landing outside the bedroom door. It was carefully made up with sheets, blankets and cover in the correct position and neatly tucked in. On top of the bed, all Susan's toys and dolls were placed in two rows about eighteen inches apart and six inches from one another. They were allowed to remain there by Michael and Anne for us to see for ourselves. It was quite bizarre. After that we were given the details, first in the spoken word and then, on my request, in writing. Michael has given me a small notebook describing the events with the dates from 26 April to 24 May 1985. I will not attempt to refer to all the things that took place in that house in one month but some of them may be of interest.

Susan's bed was returned to its room by the "poltergeist" and left neatly arranged. A sharp serrated knife from the kitchen was plunged into Michael's and Anne's bed on Anne's side. The blade was bent with the force used. All meat from the refrigerator in a wire basket was placed on their bed. Their wardrobe was placed face down on the bedroom floor and contents scattered. A calendar was taken off the wall and rolled up. Pictures were turned upside-down. All books in a bookcase had been removed and were placed neatly on top. Every single item (toothbrushes, soap, towels etc.) was removed from the bathroom and placed in the airing cupboard. The vacuum cleaner was perched neatly and dangerously on the banister of the landing. A record-player was removed and found later in the shed near the duck-house. A Royal Albert tea set on a tray on the dresser disappeared and was found later in the long grass unharmed. At times the lights in the house were swinging from the ceiling, all the doors in the house were slamming and the dog was getting very agitated and upset. A hot waterbottle, missing for days, suddenly "appeared" on Anne's upraised knees while she was reading in bed! Anne was hit on the back by a flying beaker that came in from the adjacent room.

Michael describes his arriving by car with two friends. Anne was in the porch and coming out to welcome them. As he looked at her Michael saw what he thought was a white bird flying over her head. Suddenly it fell to the ground and broke into pieces. It was a disused white teapot that had been on a shelf in the kitchen. It had "flown" from the kitchen through the living-room and porch and out into the yard where it hovered above Anne and then fell to the ground.

All these events pointed to one thing. This was a classic case of poltergeist activity. Having begun as a haunt in which a spirit was put to rest, there developed in the same home severe poltergeist activity. The question arises: "What can be done about it?"

A further example

Another case of poltergeist activity which I investigated took place in a home near Ballyclare, Co Antrim. It was a modern house occupied by a family of three persons - a husband and wife and their son who was approaching his teen years. The Rector of the Parish invited me to come and advise him as he sought to minister to a family who lived in his parish. I decided to visit the home with the Rector's permission and hear for myself what was happening.

The story was similar to what I have come to expect where there is poltergeist activity. This respectable and good family were greatly perplexed and disturbed by what they were experiencing. It started with lights going on and off for no apparent reason. Naturally, they assumed that there was something wrong with the electricity supply system, but what puzzled them most was that the light shades hanging from the ceiling were swinging backwards and forwards. Indeed this swinging was so violent at times that the light shades were leaving marks on the ceiling.

Naturally, Mr and Mrs A. decided to call in an electrician to inspect the lights of the house but he could find nothing wrong. A few days later all the lights in the house went off again so the electrician returned. This time he discovered that all the switches at the meter were turned off and in his opinion it was impossible for them to switch themselves off automatically. Someone must have done it. To ensure that no human hand could get near the switches, it was decided to secure the cupboard by putting a padlock on the door. The only key was then given to the electrician to keep.

Soon the lights went off again and as the electrician was the only one with a key, Mr A. sent for him to come and investigate. When he came and opened the cupboard door, he found all four main switches off! The electrician was baffled and Mr and Mrs A. were getting concerned.

Things got worse. Strange things began to happen to the furniture. A large wardrobe had fallen across a bed in one of the bedrooms. When I examined the wardrobe, now restored to its usual position, I found that it was heavy and steady and firmly placed against a wall. There was no natural explanation for its fall forward across the bed. Mrs A. added that as soon as they replaced the wardrobe, a chair fell across the bed and again there was no natural explanation. When the chair was put back and they were leaving the room, the chair fell across the bed a second time.

Things were hotting up. Coming out of the bedroom and on to the landing they found that a tall plant table had fallen forward and the plant sitting on it had fallen to the ground. In the toilet room, a small three-legged stool, having been removed from its usual position, sat in front of the toilet door. In their son's bedroom, various items (including Easter eggs) which had been on the top of a wardrobe were on the floor. Downstairs, a picture had fallen from a wall and another picture was turned upside-down.

A very unusual feature in this case of poltergeist activity was the arrival of the fire brigade but there was no fire. No-one in the house had sent for it. When the telephone call was traced by the fire brigade it was found to have come from their telephone! Everyone in the house denied making it.

Poltergeist activity, like severe demonisation, seems to be a rare phenomenon in this part of the world. Ministering to those who are troubled by it requires a special method of approach. I will deal with that in part 2.

Chapter Six

Some Case Histories

Some of the cases of spirit activity that I will describe in this chapter are stranger than fiction. I will confine myself to those cases in which I have been personally involved. I see no reason for reciting stories of events that have happened to others. Readers will find many such stories in the bibliography at the back of the book.

The Jeweller's Shop Spirit

In the autumn of 1992 I was asked to visit a jeweller's shop in a provincial town in Co. Antrim. The business had been in the family for sixty years. For some time prior to our visit, there had been a series of very strange happenings. It was akin to poltergeist activity. Objects were being moved from one place in the shop to another and would be found days or weeks later in unusual or inappropriate places. This was a source of considerable annoyance and anxiety in a jeweller's shop where there were so many valuable things in store and on display. The owner's handbag and purse would disappear and be later found behind boxes at the back of the shop. Pieces of jewellery left on a large working table for a few minutes would disappear, to be found later in cupboards or drawers or high shelves.

Every year about Christmas time when the staff were very busy, there was a mysterious increase of noise at the back of the shop. Boxes would be removed from the shelves and placed elsewhere. No member of the staff had done it. Nothing was stolen.

On one occasion the son of the shop owners, who was an engraver, sat working at a table at the back of the shop. Without warning or explanation the boxes on the shelves began to fly around him as if thrown by an unseen hand.

These events became such a regular feature of the shop that commercial travellers who visited the shop and knew its history were careful not to leave any valuable items on the work table unattended. They were known to disappear. It was generally accepted by them and the owners that there was something strange about the shop. What was going on was not natural.

I brought a team with me to investigate the situation. We carried out an exorcism standing round a large table at the back of the shop and using it as an altar table.

I remember two things that happened which may or may not have a natural explanation. They are amusing as we look back. One was a distinct knock on the side of the table away from me, where a member of the team was standing. That happened in a period of silence before the Service began and produced a wry smile on the faces of all, as we looked at the one standing nearest to the knock! The other strange thing was what I heard just after the opening prayer, when we asked the Father to cause the troublesome spirit to join us at the Eucharist where we would "proclaim the Lord's death" by which alone we come to salvation and receive eternal life. My back was to an open door with stairs leading up to it. At that point I heard a noise resembling footsteps coming up the stairs. None of the others heard it. Whether there was any objective reality to what I thought I heard, I do not know, but it was enough to make the hairs on the back of my neck bristle!

The main thing to consider is the result of our visit. All the strange activity ceased immediately. It was so marked that the story found its way into the local newspaper and the owners are still rejoicing in the peace of their shop today.

We have learnt since our visit that about a hundred years ago this house was used as a doctor's surgery, where operations were carried out. That may be significant.

The Lazy Ghost

In 1993 I was asked to investigate strange happenings in a small house in south-east Belfast. The couple who had lived there for five years were of good Presbyterian stock. They worshipped regularly and lived out their faith according to sound Christian principles. They were approaching old age gracefully and were looking forward to their years of retirement.

For some time the lady of the house, who took pride in keeping it spick and span, noticed that the bedclothes which she was careful to leave smooth and tidy every morning, were ruffled and disturbed in the afternoon. It appeared as if someone or something had been lying on the bed. As there were no animals in the house she kept asking her husband, "Were you lying on the bed?" Her husband's reaction to this constant query was to tell her that her imagination was over-working. He writes, "My wife would ask almost daily if I had been in the bedroom for there were creases on the bedcover, like someone had lain there. For a long time I didn't pay a lot of attention but one day when she asked,

I went in and found as she had said. Then one night my wife got up and went down the stairs. I was lying half asleep when I felt this weight slowly descending on me. It was uncanny and it happened several times after that, particularly on Sunday nights. It got to the stage when we sat and dozed in the living room on Sunday nights, maybe climbing into bed at 6.00 am. I used to say my prayers in the bathroom before retiring and often a coldness started at my ankles and proceeded up my back to my head. On other occasions my wife and I felt like something touching our heads." That is a written account from Mr R, which he wrote on my request after the exorcism had been successfully carried out. It concludes with the words, "Eventually, I was put in touch with Canon Lendrum of Lisburn Cathedral who very kindly conducted a Service of Exorcism and from that time we were not troubled."

That account can be supplemented from the notes we made when we were assessing the situation. According to the notes, both Mr and Mrs R. experienced coldness when they were praying in the bathroom or bedroom. The weight that Mr R. experienced as he lay in bed was experienced on several occasions but not quite as heavy. The weight was described to us as "something very cold". While spending Sunday nights in the living room there was the occasional sound of the bathroom door opening and footsteps walking across the bedroom floor. When things got unbearable Mr and Mrs R sought help and "two ministers offered prayer over the bed but nothing cleared." (quotation from our notes).

Mr R. contacted the previous occupants of the house to see if they had suffered in the same way. They said there was "a bad feeling" in the house. They had a constant sense of being followed. Further investigation revealed that a former resident of the house next door was a money lender and played with a ouija board on Sunday evenings. That may be significant.

The Blob Spirit

One of the most satisfying exorcisms in which I have been involved took place about 1997. It was so, not just because it was successful but because of the blessing it proved to be to the family caught up in a series of unhappy events. The mother of the family had suffered at least three miscarriages. The older child, a boy of four years, was proving to be extremely difficult, having tantrums and rebelling with great force. The younger child, a girl of two years, was severely handicapped and was not expected to survive, according to the medical profession.

It seems to me, that certain families bring into the world with them psychical gifts or tendencies. I have discovered that while dealing with those who are experiencing paranormal activity. Some people can "see" things that others cannot see. I do not believe that there is anything wrong with those who have psychic ability. If this gift is inherited from parents or grandparents there is nothing essentially evil about it. It is a gift that should be offered to God and used by those who are infilled by the Holy Spirit to the glory of God.

The mother of this afflicted family seems to have received such a gift from her mother and passed it on to her little children. My reason for saying so will become clear as I tell this story.

The older child, when he was three years old, talked again and again about another child in the house. Such a phenomenon is not unusual for children so I will not press this side of the story. What has to be taken seriously is what the child's mother said she "saw". She described it as a "hideous thing like a black blob". What she was trying to portray to us was that this "creature" had a face with a small body like a "black blob". The "black blob" was also seen on occasions both by her mother and her brother when they were babysitting for her in her home. On one occasion it appeared at the side of the baby's cot. The baby had a supply of oxygen because of a severe asthmatic condition and you can imagine the sheer horror and fear that both parents experienced when the cord of the oxygen mask was discovered, wrapped round the baby's throat three times. The older child maintained on several occasions that a "monster" had pushed him off the bed.

As well as these events that struck terror into the hearts of the parents, other things began to happen. Electric gadgets switched themselves off and on. Banging and crashing came from inside a wardrobe. A box in the attic was found to have opened without human hands. A bible reading tape stopped mysteriously in mid-sentence without any known cause. This thing was evil. It was time to seek help.

Where else could one look for help to combat this evil but from the Church? They called their Presbyterian Minister who got in touch with Brother David Jardine who asked me to investigate. Four of us went to that home and celebrated the Holy Communion together. The demon was exorcised. The result was much more than neutralising all paranormal activity. The house was cleansed, the family restored to peace, the little boy healed from his tantrums, the little handicapped girl noticeably improved, the mother happily looking forward to her third child and faith increased amongst those whom the Lord has blessed.

An Assembly of Spirits

This is a case that seems to have everything that you could have in a good ghost story. It concerns two people from Co. Fermanagh.

The house was bought about 1988 by Harold and Winifred (not their real names). From the beginning Winifred experienced strange feelings about the place. At times she heard noises that were inexplicable - rattling and clattering. Things took a serious turn one evening. Harold was in bed and Winifred was watching television. She got up to investigate a noise on the stairs and saw what she thought was a man looking over the banister rail. At first she thought it was Harold but realised it was not when she discovered that he was fast asleep in bed. On another occasion she reported seeing a figure in the garden and on investigation found no one there.

In time Harold and Winifred separated and Maureen became Harold's friend. From that time there was a series of events which convinced everyone in the house and those who came to sleep there, that there were things happening that could not be explained in natural terms. Harold's grown up son found it almost impossible to sleep because he was convinced there was a spirit in the house. During the night, doors that were difficult to open were flung wide, footsteps on the stairs and landing could be heard throughout the night, banging and clanging noises could be heard downstairs.

A number of family friends came for a short stay overnight at Christmas time - about five or six people. One of the guests saw the figure of a lady, another had the sensation of someone walking over her legs when she was in bed and another said she heard singing and music.

Of course, some of these things may have had a natural cause or were the product of a lively imagination. Who knows? Natural or not, Harold's son had enough. He decided to move out and Maureen decided to employ a medium. Whilst I would not approve of going to a medium, it is interesting to note what the medium said, after visiting the house. She claimed to "sense" that the house was a meeting place for several spirits and some of them were hostile.

There are several other events worthy of note. Both Harold and Maureen claimed to "see" figures, mostly of women and sometimes two at a time. On one occasion, when painting and decorating a bedroom, they were almost overcome by a foul smell, "like the stench of rotting animals". (Maureen's words). On another occasion, Maureen experienced a terrible coldness as soon as she began to re-arrange furniture in one of the rooms. Someone or something was making life difficult for her. To all of this there was added the constant noise at night which made sleep difficult, sometimes impossible.

A detail which may be significant, was a remark by Harold that his estranged wife owned "three unusual dolls". He admitted that he thought there was something evil about them, and that he burnt them after an argument. He divulged no further details and we did not press him on the matter. As I look back on our conversation, I wonder about what might have been going on.

I organised a team and we travelled to Co. Fermanagh, carried out an exorcism which was reported successful when we contacted Maureen on two subsequent occasions. There has been no further disturbance.

The Child Spirit

One of the most unusual stories that have come my way came through a representative of the Society for Psychical Research. She asked if I could do anything to help a lady in Craigavon who was concerned about a "spirit" child in her home. I had heard about this kind of thing from the well-known psychiatrist Dr Kenneth McAll, but I had never experienced it. (see Part 2 Chapter 2)

The lady who needed help we will call Mrs C.. She was an intelligent and articulate woman for whom the eternal verities were real. She practised her faith as a Roman Catholic, going to Church and observing other Christian duties. She was a woman of remarkable faith. If she had not been, she would not have looked for spiritual help in the way that she did. She was a young woman with a young family, the youngest being a baby of four months.

Mrs C. was seeking help because she and the whole family were conscious of the presence in the house of a "spirit child" of about two or three years old. He was seen by both her husband and herself and by at least one of the children who had seen and heard him in the bathroom. He had gone into the children's bedrooms and on one occasion he had slapped one of the children. There had been various poltergeistic effects in the kitchen - pots and pans moved and other things upset. On one occasion, she had unknowingly taken this child's hand thinking he was one of her own and led him up the stairs in the dark. When she got to the top of the stairs, she realised she was holding the hand of the phantom child. He had become an accepted member of her family when he "appeared". This will sound weird to most people, but I can only tell it as it was told to me.

Mrs C. insisted that she was not frightened by the spirit child. She was merely concerned that this child had lost his way and should not be left to wander here on earth. He needed help to move on to the next stage on his journey and to the better place where the Lord would want him to be. Shades of Dr McAll? He would have described this child as one of the "unquiet dead". In Mrs C.'s mind there was a connection between this child and a young nephew who had died a little while ago.

A few days before we arrived, Mrs C.'s mother had been babysitting for her. She too "heard" this child - a voice "mumbling" and a child-like "giggle". The children were also aware of his presence and were beginning to complain about the "baby" who disturbed them.

We had a larger team than usual with us when we arrived at Mrs C.'s home - including Jan, a curate at Lisburn Cathedral and a friend. I wondered what they thought about this bizarre situation.

I decided to celebrate the Eucharist in the home with the intention of releasing this child's spirit to God and to the place where the Lord would have him be. Whether it is called a Requiem or an Exorcism does not matter. The only important thing is that God's "will be done on earth as it is in heaven". The reaction of Mrs C. was striking and should teach us all a salutary lesson. When the Service was concluded she wept. Why? Not because we had failed in what we were attempting to do but because she knew we had succeeded. She had lost this child. He had gone to a better place. For his sake she had done her duty. She had done what she knew she ought to do and now she was suffering a kind of bereavement. Those tears of sorrow were mingled with tears of joy for she knew in her heart that the child was now at rest.

A playful spirit?

In March 1997 I was asked by a Rector to visit one of his parishioners who was experiencing strange things taking place in her home. Thelma (not her real name) was a bright and lively girl, a single parent with one child Jack of three years old. She lived in a modern council house. Mysterious things began to happen in December 1996. It started one day about 1.30 am. Thelma was wakened by the noise of Jack's spaceship - a loud buzzing sound and flashing lights. When she went into Jack's bedroom she noted several things. Jack was in bed and fast asleep, just as she had left him. The spaceship was in the "on" position, the other toys which had been tidied away were pulled out and scattered over the floor and the room was "stone cold". From that time on, several inexplicable things took place from time to time. Folded clothes that Thelma had put on Jack's bed were mysteriously moved and thrown elsewhere. Various items began to disappear, to be found later in unusual places. A clay mask which hung from a nail on the wall was found broken on the floor six feet away from where it should be lying if it fell accidentally. The nail was still in place. Jack referred constantly to a "white lady" who came to visit him from time to time. He called her "the white fairy".

Things took a more serious turn which prompted Thelma to seek help. Jack pleaded with his mum to bath him in the kitchen sink. He liked to sit there and play with his toys. Thelma left him for three minutes, playing with his toys while she went upstairs. Suddenly she was horrified to hear the spaceship. How did he get out of the sink? She rushed down to find Jack in the sink fast asleep, held upright by his ear resting on the water-tap. Drowning was a distinct possibility.

Having heard this story I decided to take for granted that these various manifestations might well spring from the presence of a spirit in this simple home of a young mother and her baby son, so I carried out an exorcism.

I contacted Thelma two weeks later and was told that there had been no further paranormal activity. Her Rector confirmed three years later that there had been no inexplicable incidents since.

It was her Rector who had contacted me and invited me to investigate the situation.

A persistent Spirit

In most cases that I have investigated, there has been little emphasis on what has been seen. Apparitions have been few. The case I am going to describe is based largely on the persistent appearance of a "lady" in various parts of the house but particularly in one bedroom. The story concerns a Belfast family in the North of the city. It was a family that impressed me by their sincerity, faith and concern for one another. By the time we arrived plans were being made to move out of the house, such was the fear that had been generated by the constant sighting of an apparition.

It is such a remarkable case that I've asked the owner and occupier of the house to write the story as she recalled it from a few years ago. I am glad to report that she is still living in the house today and is happy in the knowledge that a spirit is no longer present.

Mrs E.'s account

"My son C. was ten years old when it happened. He came running to tell me he saw a lady in the bedroom. She was old, stooped and bent over with hair falling over her face. I did not believe him at first and thought he was having a bad dream. He insisted that he was not sleeping when he saw the lady for he had had to run past her. I was still not convinced until his older sister M., who was fifteen years old told me a similar story. Her claim was that someone was talking to her when she was lying in bed. Although I had heard or seen nothing up to this point, I began to get concerned. Next day I went to the Sacred Heart Church and asked that a priest would come and say prayers of blessing in the house. He came that evening and I felt much better after he left. On the following day I met with my sister-in-law who told me she had been talking to the priest. The priest told her, although he had not told me, that he had seen the "lady" in the bedroom and "felt" her presence in the house. He advised that the children and I should stay for a while with my sister-in-law until he found out more. After a few days he came back and told me that the "lady" in my house was called Kitty Black and was a "lost soul" and needed help. He assured me there was no need to be frightened.

Things were quiet for a few weeks. C., my son, who was the first to see the "lady" was still nervous and refused to sleep alone. Then things began to happen again. I was lying in bed, wide awake, when I heard talking at the side of my bed. It was a lady's voice but I could not hear what was being said. Then my bed began to shake. I was terrified. After that things began to happen in earnest. Lights would be turned on and off. Loud noises came from upstairs. Our dog seemed to sense "something". He would sit up alert with ears erect, looking at the door. Eventually he refused to eat. I had the awful feeling that someone was watching me.

M., my daughter had the worst fright of all when she disobeyed me. I went to Manchester for a week and made arrangements for her to stay with her grandmother. On the night before I was due home, she begged her grandmother to allow her to sleep at home. She said she would sleep downstairs on the sofa and that she did. When the light was turned off for a while, M. saw the "lady" again with arms outstretched towards her. M.'s own words were "she flew at me". M. pulled the covers over her head and waited. When she lowered them the lady was still there and leaning over her. M. jumped off the sofa, switched on the lights and sat up all night.

Next day, I arrived home, but M. was afraid to tell me what had happened for she knew that I would be "mad" at her for staying there alone. That very evening the loud banging upstairs started again. It was still daylight. I was sitting downstairs on a chair beside the window and looking out. When I turned round there "she" was, standing and looking towards the door. Then she vanished. I was very frightened. That's when I got in touch with you."

So ends Mrs E.'s account of what happened. The unusual feature of this haunt is the naming of the spirit by the priest. How he discovered the name, I do not know and I have no way of finding out. I have in my possession a history of the house, going back to 1900. It has had many occupiers and amongst them there was a couple called Black. I have been told that the previous owners of the house before Mrs E. bought it knew about the presence of a spirit in the house but said nothing about it.

The reference by the priest to a lost soul raises some interesting questions. Obviously he did not mean that this soul was eternally lost. He was speaking about an earth- bound spirit, the spirit of someone who had died but for some reason, had got "stuck" or "tied" to its previous existence and still frequented its old, familiar places. Dr Kenneth McAll maintains that when a spirit manifests itself in one way or another, it is drawing attention to itself and may be looking for help, as the priest suggested. Occasionally, it is difficult to distinguish between an earth-bound spirit and a demonic spirit. Obviously, an earth-bound spirit is pitiable and harmless, whilst a demonic spirit is ruthless and destructive.

The earth-bound spirit requires to be released from its predicament so that it can pass on to the next stage on the journey. The demonic spirit should be cast out (ek ballo in Greek, meaning "I throw out") and despatched to its own place.

In my experience the way to do that is by celebrating the Sacrament of the Holy Communion. In one case, some will call it a Requiem and in the other an Exorcism. It matters not what you call it. What matters is that in either case God's will is done. No one can argue with that. We celebrated a Eucharist in Mrs E's home and whilst we belonged to different branches of the Christian faith, we received the Holy Communion together and rejoiced to do so. God honoured what we were doing. Mrs E.'s home has been at peace ever since. To God be the Glory.

A frustrated Spirit

When a person dies instantly in an explosion we can only speculate about what happens. Some who have had a near death experience have written about it. In nearly every case they have claimed that they were in an in between stage. It's as if they were on a journey in a tunnel towards light but turned back. It would be easy to postulate that sudden death may leave someone in that "in between" state, not realizing that he had died. Such may have been the case in the next story, but that is only speculation.

Robert (not his real name) was a passionate and fiery man who could be roused to bouts of fury when he was frustrated. In a fit of rage with his wife because she had upset him, he took himself off to the garden to give vent to his rage. There he had a massive heart attack, dying immediately. One can imagine the awful shock for his wife and family.

It was soon afterwards that his wife, Margaret (again not her real name) began to experience paranormal activity in her home. At first it took the form of a "noise" like a spaceship, which was how she described it. When she was in bed she felt someone get into bed with her and she was stricken with terror. It happened on a number of occasions and was so real that she could feel herself pushing this "body" out of her bed with all her strength and claims that she heard the "bump" on the floor when she was successful. I questioned her closely, but she was adamant that she was wide awake. Night after night, as she lay in bed, she could hear what she described as a "buzzing noise" and sensed that "someone" was near. At times, she said, she could feel a hand placed on her head when she was in bed.

Her daughter, who lived with her husband in her home a few miles away, also sensed what she believed was her father's presence in her home, but she was not frightened. Indeed, the feeling that her father whom she loved very much was near, gave her comfort and assurance. It was in her daughter's house that things came to a head for Margaret. While she was in her daughter's house alone, a picture on the wall began to shake and shudder violently with no one near it. That was the thing that convinced her that she needed help, so I was called and asked to investigate the situation.

Certain things need to be said about those who shared their story with me. They are intelligent people, not given to superstition or delusion. They are sound in body and mind and have been good church people of strong faith all their lives. Indeed Margaret's daughter plays a leading part in the life of her church. After I celebrated the Holy Communion in Margaret's home there was no further disturbance. It is understandable that many people will find it difficult to accept this story at face value. Some will put forward theories that seek to explain what was happening. Psychiatrists will claim to have the answer, and who am I to question what they say? However, there are two things that cannot be denied. Someone was terrified by what she was experiencing in her home and the ministry of the church brought peace.

Part 2 - The Christian Response to the Paranormal

This part is addressed mainly to clergy and Church leaders and to those who may be interested in knowing what the Christian response to the paranormal is.

I have tried to show how I have dealt with various cases of paranormal activity. I recognise that my method is not, by any means, the only way to proceed. By study and prayer, seeking the Spirit's guidance and exercising the authority conferred on the Church by Jesus Christ, I have followed a procedure that has evolved over the years and has worked for me. It has proved to be efficacious in many instances. I pass it on to my fellow clergy and ministers in the hope that they will find it helpful as they seek to minister to suffering people.

I recognise that I have not dealt with the paranormal in depth. Many have dug more deeply than I have or could. I hope I have written enough to encourage some of my fellow clergy to undertake this ministry for the sake of those in need. The important thing in any situation is not the depth of our knowledge or the breadth of our experience. The important thing is to know that we have been called and that our calling is backed by the authority of Jesus Christ.

Chapter One
The Teaching and Practice of Jesus

Most people who believe in the existence of a personal devil and an army of malevolent spirits under his authority and in his service, do so because they are taught that in Holy Scripture. For Christians, that means the Bible. In both the Old and New Testaments there are references to Satan and evil spirits. He is called by many names: Satan, meaning adversary; devil, meaning accuser or slanderer; Beelzebul (from Baal-zebub) interpreted "lord of flies." There are many other names given to Satan in the New Testament: angel of light, dragon, evil one, god of this world, prince of the power of the air.

By far the greater number of references to Satan or the devil is in the gospels. From the beginning of his ministry, Jesus is in conflict with the devil. After his baptism in the Jordan, when he was anointed with the Holy Spirit, Jesus went into the wilderness to pray and seek God's will for his life's work and there he was tempted by the devil. As soon as he began that work he came face to face with demonic activity.

> "Just then a man in their synagogue who was possessed by an evil spirit cried out, 'What do you want with us, Jesus of Nazareth? Have you come to destroy us? I know who you are - the Holy One of God!' 'Be quiet!' said Jesus sternly. 'Come out of him!'" The evil spirit shook the man violently and came out of him with a shriek."
>
> (Mark 1.23-26)

Further on in the same chapter it is recorded

> "That evening after sunset, the people brought to Jesus all the sick and demon-possessed. The whole town gathered at the door, and Jesus healed many who had various diseases. He also drove out many demons, but he would not let the demons speak because they knew who he was." (Mark 1.32-34)

Throughout the gospels, Jesus is portrayed casting out demons. Not only does he do it himself, but he gives the apostles and other disciples authority and power to do the same.

The Acts of the Apostles, which relates what happened after Jesus ascended to heaven, continues the story. It contains accounts of his disciples casting out evil spirits.

"Crowds gathered also from the towns around Jerusalem bringing their sick and those tormented by evil spirits, and all of them were healed." (Acts 5.16)

Philip the deacon conducted a successful preaching mission in the city of Samaria and it is recorded that many people were delivered of evil spirits in that city.

"With shrieks, evil spirits came out of many, and many paralytics and cripples were healed." (Acts 8.7)

In Philippi there was a girl with "a spirit by which she predicted the future" (Acts 16.16). She was constantly interrupting Paul's preaching. "Those men are the servants of the Most High God who are telling you the way to be saved. She kept this up for many days." He had tolerated her for many days but in the end he saw it as something that was hindering the Lord's work. Finally, he turned his attention to the girl who was following him and shouting out. He spoke to the spirit, not to the girl.

"Finally, Paul became so troubled that he turned round and said to the spirit, 'In the name of Jesus Christ I command you to come out of her!' At that moment the spirit left her."

There are several other references to Satan and evil spirits in the Acts of the Apostles. The epistles contain the same teaching. There is Paul's well-known account of spiritual warfare.

"Finally, be strong in the Lord and in his mighty power. Put on the full armour of God so that you can take your stand against the devil's schemes. For our struggle is not against flesh and blood, but against the rulers, against the authorities, against the powers of this dark world and against the spiritual forces of evil in the heavenly realms". (Ephesians 6.10-12)

The apostle Peter warns against the prowling and rampant enemy.

"Your enemy the devil prowls around like a roaring lion, looking for someone to devour. Resist him, standing firm in the faith."

(1 Peter 5.8)

John writes:

> "The reason the Son of God appeared was to destroy the devil's work."
> (1 John 3.8)

These are only a few of the many texts in the New Testament that refer to man's great spiritual enemy.

Today there are many Christians (including clergy of various standing) who would explain this concept of a personalised evil as the thought pattern of a primitive society. At one time I might have said the same thing. We have a western world view which militates against everything supernatural in our thinking. It can be summed up in the words, "We can't believe that these days!"

Michael Green, in his book "I believe in Satan's Downfall" writes, "It would be broadly true to say that disbelief in the devil is a characteristic only of materialistic Western Christendom."

No one spoke more persistently about the devil and his works than Jesus. In the Old Testament there are few references to man's great spiritual adversary. Suddenly, when Jesus comes on the scene, Satan is thrust into centre stage. Was Jesus mistaken? If modern theological professors and psychological teachers are right, then Jesus was terribly wrong. How can this be explained? Only in one of two ways. Either he did not believe what he said, or he was a child of his age and went along with the generally held beliefs of his day. The first idea that Jesus did not mean what he said and did not mean it to be taken literally is so absurd that ordinary Christians will not want to spend time arguing about it.

The other proposition that Jesus was a child of his age deserves examination. Three things need to be said.

1. It was not usual for Jesus to accept uncritically everything that he was taught. In fact the opposite was true. He was not a conformist or a traditionalist, which was the very thing that called down upon his head the wrath of the chief priests, scribes and Pharisees and ultimately led to the cross. Far from being a child of his age, he was, in a very real sense, the father of his age. He followed his own beliefs. He was his own man. He taught with his own authority and not as the scribes. He did not follow slavishly what he heard and learnt from others. He went his own way. And when his teaching and practice became so much wrapped up in, and involved with, demonic activity he was not being a child of his age. He was going beyond that and demonstrating in a way and to an

extent that no man had ever done before him, that demons were real and active in the world.

2. Every part of Jesus' life and ministry was bound up with the conception of the reality of Satan's existence and activity in the world. His birth, teaching, ministry of healing and death were bound up with it. The story of his infancy is one of several attempts on His life. (Matthew 2.13-16). When he went to Nazareth those who heard him tried to kill him (Luke 4.28, 29). In the wilderness as he prayed for guidance and strength to know and to do his Father's will, Satan tried to divert Him. (Luke 4.13).

All the attempts that were made by Satan to destroy Jesus failed, until he was ready to face the cross. The beginning of the event that led to the cross of Jesus took place in the upper room when one of his own disciples became a tool in Satan's hands to betray him to the chief priests. The words are shockingly plain. "As soon as Judas took the bread Satan entered into him. 'What you are about to do, do quickly' Jesus told him. He went out and it was night."

3. If we regard Jesus as a child of his age in things relating to Satan and demonic activity, is he not also a child of his age in his teaching about God? Can we pick and choose the things that we like from his life and teaching and leave the other things to one side? Is what he said about God, prayer, ethical standards, heaven, hell, human relationships, to be cherry-picked?

Michael Green writes, "The fact that Jesus taught so clearly the existence of Satan is the most powerful reason for his followers to take the same stance and act accordingly." For Christians, Jesus must remain the supreme authority in these matters. Professors of theology who claim to be expounding the teaching of Jesus or psychiatrists (many of whom do not accept the teaching of Jesus) may have their own thoughts and ideas about spiritual realities. I understand their problems and queries. Like most of those who will read this book they have been brought up with a western scientific world view and because of that world view, all of us have similar difficulties.

However, having served God in the ministry of the Church for more than fifty years, and having come face to face with various forms of paranormal activity, I find it equally difficult to deny the existence of things that are beyond my understanding. Is it scientific to be dogmatic about something because it is beyond our understanding? My appeal to those who find it hard to accept the plain teaching of Jesus is to consider what he said and did in a spirit of openness. For Christians he remains the ultimate authority. To reject his plain teaching about heaven, the existence of a spiritual enemy, demonic activity, spiritual warfare because it is hard to accept or understand, is to dilute "the medicine of the gospel."

Almighty God,
You called Luke the physician
Whose praise is in the gospel,
To be an evangelist
And physician of the soul:
Give your Church, by the grace of the Spirit
And through the medicine of the Gospel,
The same love and power to heal:
Through Jesus Christ, our Lord
Amen.

(Collect of Saint Luke's day)

Chapter Two
Exercising Authority

Iimagine that most of us can remember an event in our lives which marked a distinct change of direction. We may not have realised it at the time but what appeared to be a mere chance encounter made a difference that lasted a lifetime.

I recall two such events in my life. The first was that Saturday in 1972 when I went shopping with my wife. It was not my favourite occupation. We parked the car outside a Belfast public library and while I was waiting for my wife to return with her goods, I decided to take a quick run round the library and see if I could find a book on the subject of the Holy Spirit. At that time there was great emphasis and much discussion about the person and work of the Holy Spirit. I could not find a book that impressed me but as I left the library I noticed a book sitting on a shelf. Obviously it had not yet been borrowed. It was a brand new book. I lifted it out of curiosity to look at the title and I read: "Did you receive the Holy Spirit?"

The book was written by the Rev. Simon Tugwell, a Dominican Priest. Reading that book, I discovered a new and refreshing experience of the Holy Spirit. It is not necessary for me to go into the details of exactly what happened. All I need to say is that my life was changed and my ministry was transformed. I know too, as I look back on that important day in my life, that as a result of what happened to me, other lives have been touched and renewed by the power of the Holy Spirit. It's a sobering thought, that what seemed to be an ordinary and commonplace event, caused a rippling effect on other lives that is still going on today.

Another event that shaped my ministry for the past thirty years was a short visit I made to a meeting in Stranmillis College in 1974. An international healing conference, organised by the Rev F.A. Baillie, was taking place and speakers from far and near were addressing the conference. I was not a delegate but I took the opportunity to attend a lecture given by Dr Kenneth McAll on the theme: "The Ministry of Deliverance." I was interested in the subject but knew little about it. That lecture proved to be a turning point in my ministry.

Dr McAll is a well-known surgeon and psychiatrist. The son of congregationalist missionaries, he was a man of deep Christian faith. As a surgeon, he went to practise in China in the mid thirties. It was there he had an experience which changed his life. Being a doctor and a scientist he was sceptical of anything that savoured of the paranormal. For him, nature was a closed system and everything in it was a matter of cause and effect. For him things needed to be investigated and demonstrated scientifically before he could accept them.

In the first chapter of his book "Healing the Family Tree" he describes what happened to him in China. He writes:

"One evening as the sun was shining I was tramping along a dusty road...Suddenly I was surprised by a man dressed entirely in white, who came up behind me. Pointing to a village away along a track at right angles to the one we were on, he told me that there were many wounded people there needing my help. At first, I thought he was just a misguided farmer returning home late, but his urgency persuaded me to change direction and I went with him to his village. The gates were thrown open and I was pulled inside, but the man was nowhere to be seen. The villagers told me that I had narrowly avoided a Japanese ambush, as the hospital that had been my destination was now over run. They questioned me closely about my change of direction and knowledge of their wounded and insisted that no one from the village had been outside the walls that day. I remembered that the white-robed stranger had spoken to me in English and I was certainly the only foreigner within miles. I knew then that it was Jesus who had appeared to me."

For theological reasons I would interpret this divine intervention as the visitation of an angel to Dr McAll, directing his footsteps away from danger to where he was much needed. There are many such stories today, testifying to the ministry of angels, guiding and protecting people who are moving in the wrong direction or into danger. Angels are real and active today as they were in the life and times of Jesus.

The effect on Dr McAll was to re-assess his previously held conviction that Chinese beliefs about spirits, exorcism and the supernatural were mere superstition. He writes:

"I was struggling helplessly with the psychosomatic illnesses of my patients. Finally, I gave in. In 1956 I decided that I must investigate psychiatric diseases. I went back to university, specialised in psychiatry and lived in mental hospitals..."

After the Conference at Stranmillis College, I received a telephone call from Dr Paddy McEvoy. Dr McAll would like to meet a group of clergy in Dr McEvoy's home. Could I come? I was honoured to be asked and was glad to accept.

That meeting touched me deeply and had a profound effect on my life. It started about 8.00 pm and we were still there, a dozen clergy from various denominations, till after 3.00 am. Dr McAll talked for most of that time about his faith and experiences of bringing healing to people by, what I will call, spiritual means. His faith and sincerity were unquestionable. As he told story after story, his voice would break with emotion and tears would flow. In his book "Healing the Family Tree" many of those stories are told and his teaching and methods are clearly stated.

I would be less than honest if I were to say that I have accepted everything that Dr McAll writes about healing. However, the faith and sincerity of the man, together with his dedication and the effectiveness of his work, is beyond question. The debt I owe to him is what I learnt that evening about the Deliverance Ministry. He showed me the precious gift that Jesus gave to the Church when he instituted the sacrament of the Holy Communion. It is ironic that I, an anglican priest, came to appreciate the power of the Eucharist through the son of Congregationalist missionaries.

The thrust of his teaching on the Ministry of Deliverance is that it should take place in the context of the Eucharist. Earthbound spirits can be released by the authority and power of Jesus Christ manifested at a Eucharist. Evil spirits can be bound and despatched to the place appointed for them by Jesus Christ. People and places can be freed and set free of every evil presence and disturbance. That is why it is my custom to celebrate the Holy Communion in any serious attempt at the exorcism of a person or a place. I will describe later how that can be done by those ordained and appointed for this work by Our Lord Jesus Christ.

There is an authority and power in a celebration of the Eucharist that I have not found in any other rite. Again and again, I have been told by people seeking help because of the disturbing presence of a spirit in their home: "The Rector (or the Minister) came and said a prayer in the house but it made no difference." In my experience of exorcising a place, a Service of Holy Communion and a command spoken in the name of Our Lord Jesus Christ is enough to free the house of the supernatural disturbance.

God's Calling

In Christian ministry there are varieties of gifts.

"There are different kinds of gifts but the same Spirit. There are different kinds of service, but the same Lord. There are different kinds of working, but the same God works all of them in all men."

(1 Cor.12. 4-6) .

People are not called or gifted by God in exactly the same way. "All these are the work of one and the same Spirit and He gives them to each one as He determines." (1 Cor. 12.11). Those who are called to the Deliverance Ministry may be involved mostly with people and others mostly with places. That does not necessarily mean that you will be involved in one but not in the other. You will do both as God calls you. In my case, I have found that I am called mostly to deal with places. In the past 25 years I reckon that I have dealt with considerably more than 50 cases. I will describe some of these in chapter 9.

After I had begun to write this chapter, I had a telephone call from a Roman Catholic friend who was a close associate of mine in the early days of the Charismatic Renewal in the seventies. We have not seen much of each other for nearly 20 years. He is still leading a Christian community that was formed in the early days of the Renewal. He enquired if I would see a lady for whom his community had prayed many times, without apparent success. She might need to be set free from a spirit that was causing her distress. In the course of a brief conversation, he commented that it was getting increasingly difficult to find clergy who were prepared to perform this ministry. He had been able to use a priest in the past but the priest had now grown old and frail and was not able to continue any longer.

Is this not true of all churches? Having been a busy Rector, I can understand that it may not be easy for some to undertake this work. Time is not available, but is time the main stumbling block? On occasions I have sensed fear. Sometimes, I have been told, "I don't know anything about this. I'm not qualified. You do it." Two simple thoughts occur to me.

1. Jesus gave his Church authority and power to do this work. "He called His twelve disciples and gave them authority to drive out evil spirits." (Matthew 10.1). "The seventy-two returned with joy and said, 'Lord, even the demons submit to us in Your name'". (Luke 10.17). No one who takes the teaching of the New Testament seriously can doubt the authority that Jesus has given to his Church.

I recall an interview given by the former Archbishop of Canterbury, Dr Donald Coggan many years ago. It was just after an exorcism attempted by two Church of England clergymen that had gone tragically wrong. The attempt failed after an all night session. The man who was being exorcised, Michael Taylor by name, went home and murdered his wife. Many people were extremely critical and described what had been attempted as medieval nonsense. The press had a field-day. This practice must be stopped by legislation. The Archbishop was attacked fiercely by the interviewer. "Archbishop, isn't it time you put an end to this primitive practice in the Church of England?" The Archbishop's reply was plain and forthright. "I am not aware that Jesus Christ has withdrawn his commission to his Church."

If Jesus has given that commission to his Church, who should be carrying it out today? Surely it is those who have been ordained and given the authority of spiritual leadership in the Church. I believe in the grace of ordination. Paul writes to Timothy "For this reason, I remind you to fan into flame the gift of God which is in you through the laying on of my hands. For God did not give us a spirit of timidity, but a spirit of power, of love and of self-discipline." (2 Timothy 1.6). The laity may be used in this ministry as helpers, but the lead should be given by those who have been ordained and who can, where it is desirable, provide the context of the sacrament of the Holy Communion.

2. The second thought I have in mind is the method used by Jesus in the training of his disciples to minister to those in need. It was the apprentice method. Jesus ministered to those in need, while the disciples watched and helped. The disciples ministered to those in need, while Jesus watched and helped. Then the disciples were sent out in twos to minister without the physical presence of Jesus.

What better way could there be to train those who say: "I don't know anything about this. I am not qualified." Sometimes it is not a matter of being qualified or knowing. It is a matter of faith and obedience. The authority given you through the laying on of hands when you were ordained by the Bishop is the first step in being qualified. "Take thou authority..." was the commission given in the words of the old Book of Common Prayer.

Many years ago I recall a Rector asking me to minister to one of his parishioners. I cannot recall exactly what the need was except that it involved the paranormal. The Rector brought me to the house and introduced me to the family. Try to imagine my surprise when he walked out of the house and left me to my own devices! Apart from learning a little about how to deal with the situation, he missed a great opportunity for evangelism.

On another occasion I travelled nearly one hundred miles with a team of four others to minister in a home that was troubled by disturbing spirits. The Rector had kindly given me permission to minister in his parish and a day was arranged when an exorcism could be attempted. I understood that the Rector would be present. When the time came the Rector declined to come. The exorcism was successful but it was sad that an opportunity to acquire experience about how to minister in this situation was lost. Being present at a Service of Exorcism is a better way to learn about it than reading many books. This apprentice method, as it has been called, was that used by Jesus in training disciples.

Sadly, it has been my observance over the years that some clergy prefer not to be involved in something that is mysterious, ethereal and outside normal experience. Today, we need ordained men to whom people can go with confidence when they are faced with problems that may have their roots in the paranormal. Such occurrences may be rare but they do happen from time to time. If they cannot find spiritual relief and comfort from their spiritual pastors, where can they find it?

It is said that the Church of England has an official Exorcist in every diocese. His role is not to be present at every exorcism but to advise and assist when the local clergy run into difficulties. The bulk of the work should be carried out by those appointed by the Bishop to "care for the souls of the parish".

Chapter Three
The Ministry of Deliverance

When I was at college preparing for ordination in the forties the expression "ministry of deliverance" meant nothing to me. Today it seems to be the "in-thing." The Charismatic Movement has brought the reality of spiritual warfare into the centre of Christian thinking. That should not surprise anyone. During the past thirty or forty years there has been a big increase in people's interest in the supernatural. The more they have been caught up in the wave of sheer materialism the more they have turned to other philosophies in a search for spiritual reality. Subjects like the New Age Movement, transcendental meditation and other forms of Eastern religious practices have drawn them away.

Occult activity which has been defined as "a search for truth in the hidden areas of life" is more common today than it was forty years ago and such searching for truth in these ways is a serious indictment of today's church. We have failed to get our message across that Jesus is "the Light of the world" and that those who follow Him "have the light of life." We have failed to convince people that He is "the bread of life" who satisfies the deepest longings of the human heart.

If people do not find what they need in the Church, they will look for it elsewhere. The danger is that they will stray into areas that bring them into touch with spiritual entities that can lead to deep unhappiness and bring them into captivity. For these reasons the Ministry of Deliverance has become an important part of the Church's work.

The Ministry of Deliverance is a rescue mission. It's a form of ministry that aims to set people free from the presence and control of that which the New Testament calls demons or spirits. People will have different thoughts or ideas about it. Keep in mind that when I write about the Deliverance Ministry in this chapter I am NOT referring to what is sometimes called major exorcism. I define it as minor exorcism.

The word minor does not mean the Ministry of Deliverance is unimportant or insignificant. No form of exorcism should be approached casually. It's a serious business and must be handled with the utmost care and sensitivity. Just as a surgeon regards every operation, no matter how minor, as serious and takes the utmost care that no harm will come to his patient, so the Christian Minister, undertaking the Ministry of Deliverance, will consider prayerfully how he should proceed. I must, therefore, begin with a note of caution. Three things need to be said.

First, this practice of performing a Deliverance Ministry should not become so common that it might be considered fashionable or the "in thing". There is a tendency to use it when we are dealing with someone who puzzles or baffles us. We rush too quickly to the conclusion that this person, who is telling his story and is asking for prayer, needs to be delivered from an evil spirit. We need to guard against the temptation to "take the easy way out" when we run out of ideas. The probability is that evil spirits are not the cause of the problem and it is wrong to declare that they are, unless you have good reason to believe so.

Second, it is a very alarming and possibly harmful thing to suggest to anyone that he or she is controlled or troubled by an evil spirit. You may have that thought in mind and you may have good reasons for thinking so, but you may be wrong.

Dr Martin Lloyd Jones tells the story of a friend of his who became ill and began to use foul language to his wife and family and all who came to see him. Everyone who heard him was amazed and baffled because the man had been a devoted servant of Jesus Christ all his life. Where did he learn such language? Such filthy words? Everyone was appalled. Dr MLJ was summoned to his bedside. His family believed their loved one was demonised and needed to be exorcised. As is well known, Dr Martin Lloyd Jones was not only a gifted preacher and Bible teacher, he was also a medical man of great repute. He saw immediately the cause of the man's problem. He was suffering from a severe chemical imbalance and required medical treatment. When he received the necessary treatment, his behaviour returned to normal. The lesson for us is plain. Strange or unusual behaviour is not necessarily caused by the presence of evil spirits.

Third, not everyone is called or gifted for this ministry. Paradoxically, those who tend to rush in to cast out evil spirits are those not trained or equipped to carry it out successfully. Sometimes it is the young, immature or enthusiastic person who rushes in where angels fear to tread. They may emerge unscathed but leave behind the one they are trying to help damaged and upset and the Church's Ministry is brought into disrepute.

Some who are interested in this ministry and feel themselves drawn to it, may be so for the wrong reasons. They need to be careful and examine their motives. It's important to ensure that they are not getting into it to satisfy curiosity or seek popularity or demonstrate power. That is not what it is about.

An important qualification

Perhaps the attribute most suited for this work is reluctance, with *a willingness to obey*. Obviously, other gifts are required such as faith, courage, leadership and authority but reluctance and a willingness to obey are a necessary safeguard against getting involved for the wrong reasons. The wise advice of C S Lewis about spirits and demons (quoted in chapter 2) should always be heeded. He counsels against two "equal and opposite errors" to avoid. One error is not to believe in their existence at all. The other error is having an unhealthy interest and fascination in them. We need to face up to the possibility that some Christians can develop an unhealthy curiosity in spirit activity. The person who sees demons under every bed can do as much damage to the witness of the Church and its healing ministry as the sceptic who believes only in what he can touch, handle and see.

Not everyone who professes to follow Christ believes in the existence of evil spirits and even those who say they do, regard such a belief as academic. It does not impinge on life in a practical way. The baptismal vow "I renounce the devil and all his works..." does not mean as much for modern man living in modern society as "I renounce...all the sinful lusts of the flesh." There is a note of unreality in the former but reality in the latter. Yet the teaching and practice of Jesus is clear as I have tried to show. As Christians we are bound to take into consideration what he, who is the supreme authority in these matters, said and did.

Those who seek the help of the Church are very unlikely to be severely demonised. If such a situation did arise, it would require expert handling by a team of experienced people who have been called and trained for this work. Such ministry would involve major exorcism which is a most unpleasant business, very rare in this country and not for the novice.

However, those who come for Christian counselling and prayer may benefit from the ministry of minor exorcism or the Ministry of Deliverance, to give it its modern and more polite name. What lies behind it is the idea that certain maladies are caused by the presence and activity of spirits. There is almost no limit to what troubles, some people believe, can be ascribed to demonic or spirit activity. They include addictions and irrational impulses, such as anger, lust, jealousy, depression and various other moods and psychological conditions.

I have no doubt that spirits can and do impinge on human life. They can play some part in causing (or, more likely worsening) the things that trouble and depress humankind but great care has to be taken not to give people the impression that they are "occupied" or "indwelt" or "possessed" or "owned" by evil spirits. There is all the difference in the world between being attacked or afflicted or oppressed by spirits from "without" and being controlled or directed or possessed by spirits from "within." Indeed it may be true to say that all of us have gone through the experience of being attacked from "without" at times and we have not realised it. The sudden row that blew up on the way out to Church! The unexpected difficulty as we do something important for the Kingdom of God! That overwhelming temptation when we thought we had conquered it! Spirits are always around to take advantage of our weaknesses.

People who can benefit from the Ministry of Deliverance are those who find difficulty in shaking off these attacks. The spirits seem to have a particular line or channel through which they can come at will. The exercise of the Ministry of Deliverance rebukes the spirit and commands it to depart, forbids it to return and seals up the channel or line that it has established into the person's life.

Let us suppose that you are involved in praying for, or ministering to someone in need. He comes to you with a psychological or spiritual problem: depression, addiction, anger, lust, hatred or some other recurring affliction. He tells you his story. What should you do?

There are several things that you can and should do.

First listen and say as little as possible. Your foremost duty is to show interest, sympathy and understanding. It may be necessary for you to give encouragement to the one who is opening his heart to you by asking leading questions. Under no circumstances should you probe beyond what the person wants to reveal and you should never register shock.

Second, look for a natural cause of the problem. Does it arise from the person's background or circumstances? Is it a weakness or trait that may have been inherited? Does it spring from a past or present relationship? Has there been some traumatic experience in the past that is very deep within? Is there a guilt problem? There is almost no end to the things you need to consider if you look for a natural cause. Indeed it may take a qualified psychiatrist to discover the things that are playing a part in someone's condition. Do not jump easily or quickly to the conclusion that there are spirits present and there is a need for the Ministry of Deliverance.

Third, love this troubled person with the love of Jesus. Any kind of ministry that does not flow out of a heart of love and compassion is not the ministry of Jesus. Ministry in his name is gentle, thoughtful and kind. Such ministry will not be marked by a "rushing in" to cast out evil spirits.

Fourth, if you believe in your heart that spirits are either the cause of the malady or are taking advantage of a natural weakness, you must look for a way to deal with the situation without distressing the individual. There is, I believe, an example of that in the life of Jesus. When he returned from the synagogue with his disciples to the house of Simon Peter on the Sabbath, he found Peter's mother-in-law sick with a fever. It was a big disappointment. They were expecting lunch. The disciples asked Jesus to help her. "So Jesus bent over her and rebuked the fever and it left her. She got up at once and began to wait on them." (Luke 4.38, 39). The word "rebuke" suggests that there was something more than fever present. Who rebukes inanimate, lifeless objects? You may thump the table but you do not rebuke it. You rebuke people or animals or whatever has conscious life and is able to hear your rebuke.

The natural interpretation of this incident is that Jesus discerned it was a spirit that afflicted her and when he rebuked the fever it (the spirit) left her. I wonder if Peter's mother-in-law ever knew that she was being afflicted by a spirit! Perhaps not. She did not need to know, to be delivered.

So here's a way of undoing the work of a spirit without distressing the one you are trying to help. Address the malady! Rebuke it as Jesus did. Command it to go and never to return. Do this in the name and with the authority of Jesus Christ. If the malady is caused by the presence and activity of the spirit, it will leave. If not, you were wrong in your diagnosis.

In the case of someone being helped or healed by a successful ministry of "rebuking a malady" there must be a follow-up which will involve at least two things:

1. A sealing of the channel or line down which the spirit has been coming to cause pain and suffering. The sealing against the spirit's return is done by a pronouncement of authority and power in Jesus' name. "I seal off this channel that has been opened into this person's life and close it for ever against any spirit that would seek to use it, in the name and with the authority of Jesus Christ.

2. A filling of the vacuum that is now left by the departure of the spirit. (Matthew 12.43-45) Or, to use another metaphor, the building up of a defence against any further attacks. (Ephesians 6.10-11)

I recall several instances in which I used this method of bringing relief to someone who, in my judgement, was troubled on occasions by an alien presence.

The first example is of a young woman who had a problem that baffled and troubled her. She was a committed Christian and served her Lord and Church faithfully and well. From time to time, she had bouts of irrational anger. She knew that her anger was not justified. If challenged, she could give no reason for it. She explained to me that these bouts of anger started a few years earlier. She had gone through a traumatic experience that had caused her deep hurt and disappointment and from that time on she experienced periods of anger. I had witnessed this anger once but dismissed it, a little puzzled and surprised. She asked for prayer. In the course of praying for her, I pondered on what was causing these bouts of anger. Was she under attack from an alien spirit? Had something latched on to her during that time of trauma? Of course I could not be certain. I was not dealing with something that could be heard or seen or touched. Nevertheless, I was moved to assume the presence of a spirit of anger. I commanded this "spirit of anger" to leave and never to molest her again. I exercised the authority given to the Church to bind the spirit and to loose the one who wanted to be free. It was a quiet but powerful ministry, for that young woman was set free from the spirit of anger that was destroying her witness and spoiling her life.

The second example concerns a teenager who was finding things very difficult. She was a senior grammar schoolgirl but because of her unhappiness, she had transferred to a different school. Later she took an overdose and naturally her parents were greatly troubled and concerned for her. It was decided she should see a psychiatrist. One of her symptoms was hearing voices in her head and the psychiatrist thought she might be suffering from schizophrenia but another doctor was horrified at the diagnosis and rejected it. Her rector asked me to see her for he thought there was something sinister in her behaviour. My wife and I had a chat with her and we found her to be a gentle, quiet and co-operative girl, showing genuine appreciation of any help we might be able to give. During a time of prayer, I decided to "speak" to the voices that were troubling and upsetting her. I spoke with authority, commanding them to be silent and never to speak to her again. "You are to depart from her. I bind you and cast you out and you will never return to this child of God again to torment her. You will go to your own place and remain."

When the prayer time was concluded I asked the girl: "How are you now? Do you feel any different?" Her reply was: "They're gone!" I asked: "Why do you say that?" Her words were sweet music to our ears. "When you were praying" she said, "they were talking to me. But as soon as you told them to leave, they began to scream and then there was silence. They're gone!"

There is always the possibility that what seems to be a real and total healing will be shown to be bogus after a few weeks or months. In this case it proved to be absolutely genuine. After a couple of years the voices remain silent, happiness has been restored and a life set free. Medical attention is no longer necessary, medicines have been withdrawn by her doctor and a young girl is looking forward to a happy future.

The third example concerns a disturbed ten-year-old child. She was full of anger at times and was very conscious of how she felt. When a child of that age says to you "I am full of anger inside me", you have to take notice. You cannot ignore it. It was making her mother's life unbearable in public and in private.

I saw three possible reasons for this anger. It may have come from her genes. Her father had given his parents trouble when he was young. It may have come from her circumstances which were very trying and unfortunate. Or it may have had something to do with the presence of an evil spirit. She was anti-religious, anti-church and anti-God at times.

I came, rightly or wrongly, to the conclusion that all three causes operated in her condition. But the last thing I wanted to do was to convey to this intelligent child that she was being afflicted by an evil spirit. So, what was I to do?

I decided to talk with her alone. That was not easy because of her anti-religious outlook. I talked with her about how everyone has genes and that means that we can bring bad things as well as good things with us into the world. The anger she experienced inside her and that burst out in fits of rage at times was not a good thing but it was not her fault. I told her too that I was aware of her unfortunate circumstances in which she was being deprived of things that other children enjoyed and that too was making her angry. I assured her that I knew it was not her fault. Having built up a rapport with her, I told her I would like to pray with her and she raised no objection.

First, I revealed to her that I had noticed three things in her that would have to go, if she was going to be happy. (I had discerned what those three things were. They were anger, hatred and a critical spirit). So, in a short time of prayer I commanded Anger to leave. I commanded Hatred to leave. I commanded Criticism to leave. At no time did I suggest demons or evil spirits to her. I concluded by encouraging her to put her trust in Jesus who loved her. Then I laid my hands gently on her head and asked the Holy Spirit to fill her life.

She is not yet a perfect little girl. Of course not. But her mother who reports her behaviour to me on a regular basis assures me that she is remarkably improved and a very different child. She has been admitted to a grammar school, is working very hard and is doing well.

The Ministry of Deliverance is a valid part of the ministry of the Church. It needs to be exercised with compassion, wisdom and care, and always to the glory of God. When properly used it can be very effective, and people who may have been suffering for years can be set free instantaneously.

My plea is that it should be used with great care, wisdom and sensitivity. As C S Lewis has suggested, nothing would please our adversary more than that the Ministry of Deliverance should become the "in thing" in Christian Ministry. That could do more harm than good. Those who feel drawn to this ministry should receive proper training and authority from the Church.

Chapter Four
Major Exorcism

I have already made it clear that my aim is to share my experiences of the paranormal. What I write is based on what I have seen and heard in the course of many years in the Christian Ministry. I have not sought these experiences but they have come my way. Others who have travelled on the same path, may be totally oblivious of anything that savours of the unusual or mysterious or paranormal. That does not make them in any sense inferior. Everyone has his gift from God.

"There are different kinds of gifts, but the same Spirit. There are different kinds of service, but the same Lord. There are different kinds of working, but the same God works all of them in all men. Now to each one the manifestation of the Spirit is given for the common good. To one is given through the Spirit the message of wisdom, to another the message of knowledge by means of the same Spirit, to another faith by the same Spirit, to another gifts of healing by that one Spirit, to another miraculous powers, to another prophesy, to another distinguishing between spirits, to another speaking in different kinds of tongues, and to still another the interpretation of tongues. All these are the work of the one and the same Spirit and He gives them to each one just as He determines." (1 Corinthians 12.4-11)

It is not my intention to write an academic treatise on the paranormal. Many others have written on the subject.

When I write about major exorcism, I am referring to the exorcism of those who are *severely* demonized. Such exorcism should not be attempted, except by those who are called and trained for this work. It should be undertaken by a team of ministers who are backed by the authority of their Church and by prayer. This is a specialised ministry for which some have been gifted by the Holy Spirit.

Cases of severe demonisation (sometimes described as possession) are rare in this country. I have met only four. By severe demonisation I mean those cases in which demons manifest themselves outwardly by taking over a person's behaviour or speech. Sometimes they will mock, jeer, argue and say things to frighten and discourage. I stress again that the accounts of this book are about what I have seen and heard. It happened to me!

One of my more lurid experiences came some years ago when I received a telephone call from a young woman. Roberta (not her real name) had gone to her doctor, very distressed because of events that took place in her home on the previous evening. The events were so bizarre, I hesitate to describe them. They were told to me in great detail and I have several pages of notes that speak of things stranger than fiction. Obviously Roberta discussed some of these things with her doctor who passed her over to me.

It is interesting to note in passing that a doctor acknowledged the reality of what Roberta had told him and called in the assistance of the Church. Sometimes doctors are more ready than we think to concede the need for spiritual ministrations in facing problems that are outside their sphere. I recall the case of an ordained man who went to his doctor because of stress and tension as a result of what he considered to be paranormal activity in his rectory. The doctor advised him to go to his Bishop. "Why are you coming to me? Go to your Bishop. The Church should be able to deal with these things." The outcome was that the Bishop asked me to visit the rectory and together we carried out an exorcism of the place and there was no further trouble there.

To continue with the Roberta episode, I will recount the events as told to me in the presence of her partner and two friends who came with me. The story begins with an apparition. Roberta wakened early one morning and saw the figure of a lady at her bedside. She had the appearance of her grandmother who died twenty-two years previously. She was wearing a long flowing gown. Roberta heard a voice saying clearly, "Roberta, you will be the next one to be with me." The same figure appeared again to Roberta and her partner when they were watching television. The noise of footsteps was often heard coming from upstairs. Their alsatian dog shivered and cowered and refused to investigate.

The final episode is as hard for me to describe as it will be for some to accept but I can only tell it as it was told to me. Roberta was sitting on the floor watching a late night film when she began to choke. Her partner was sitting beside her and looked to see what was wrong. He saw that Roberta's face was blue and a pair of hands were gripped round her throat. I questioned him closely. "The hand" he said "was as clear as day. It ended at the wrist with a frilled cuff."

As soon as Roberta recovered, they decided that they could not stay there any longer. After they had gathered some bits and pieces together before leaving, on their way to the door they glanced back and saw the lady with the long flowing robe standing at the top of the stairs. As they closed the door behind them they heard laughter. Next morning Roberta went to her doctor. Her doctor referred her to me.

It's an incredible story and if I had not talked personally with this couple, I would find it hard to believe. What was I to do? A medical doctor had put this couple into my hands. As a Christian minister I could not walk away. I made a diagnosis of the situation, which I know now was mistaken in view of what happened later. I assumed that there was an earth-bound spirit in the house and that I should follow the steps that I would normally take to release the spirit and send it on its way to the place where the Lord would want it to be. (I will explain these steps more fully in a later chapter.)

However, this was not an earth-bound spirit, but more sinister than that. I decided to celebrate Holy Communion in the house and in that context to perform an exorcism. The word exorcism may not be the correct one to use in dealing with earth-bound spirits but it will serve for our purpose. Perhaps the word requiem might be more accurate. Neither word is found in Holy Scripture. While I was removing my surplice and replacing the Communion vessels believing that I had dealt successfully with the problem, I asked Roberta how she felt about things now. With a rather peculiar expression, she began to explain what she was experiencing. Throughout the Communion Service she had a strong urge inside her, she said, to mock and laugh. It was obvious to me as I looked at her that she was still feeling that way. She was having difficulty in keeping her desire to mock and laugh under control. She was not able to hide or control it.

Whether it was plain common sense or the operation of the gift of "distinguishing between spirits" (1 Corinthians 12.10), I saw in Roberta the presence of a mocking, hostile demon. Immediately I confronted the demon by looking closely into Roberta's eyes and challenging it. I dared it to go on mocking. Deliberately I provoked it by showing that I was not deceived or upset by it. I knew in my heart that I had the authority and power to deal with it, to cast it out and despatch it to its own place.

Suddenly and without any warning an amazing thing happened. Roberta, who was sitting on a low couch between my two friends, rose to her feet and attacked me. She was a small girl, about five feet tall and weighing about seven stone or less. I was nearly twice her weight and would have been considered at that time to be very fit, solid and strong. While I was perplexed at this assault, I was not unduly worried. Naturally, I resisted her and tried to hold her at bay but she displayed amazing strength. I was beginning to lose the battle. At one point she came very near to throwing me to the ground. It was then that I realised my mistake. I was fighting her in the flesh. I should have been fighting the demon in the power of the Spirit. So I spoke with authority (indeed I shouted), "In the name of Jesus, stop!" Those were my exact words. I could not ever forget them for they had an amazing effect. Roberta fell to the ground as if someone had hit her with a hammer and lay motionless. I leaned over her and commanded the demon to leave. As I continued to command with increasing pressure, there was a loud scream from Roberta, still lying where she had fallen. The demon left and Roberta sat up.

Like Alice (Part 1 Chapter 2) she wanted to know what had happened to her and how she came to be on the floor. She insisted on knowing, so we told her and led her in an act of faith in which she put her faith in Jesus and invited the Holy Spirit to come into her life. I visited her a few times after that and found her at peace. My visits had to cease because I found it quite impossible to travel regularly to her home and to give her the time required to establish and strengthen her in the faith. However, the Rector who was a friend of mine knew the situation and agreed to undertake a special follow up ministry. Like the great majority of clergy, he confessed that he had little knowledge or experience of demonic activity and how to deal with it. He was a good pastor and under normal circumstances would have had no difficulty. Unfortunately, the parish church to which he had just been appointed did not have a group of people who met regularly for prayer, fellowship and study and who would have been a help to Roberta in encouraging and strengthening her. Sadly, he concluded that it would be better to pass her on to another congregation.

It's my earnest hope that this important part of Christian ministry to those afflicted by demons or evil spirits will not be neglected or ignored. I pray that some will know themselves called and gifted by God for this work and seek the knowledge and training necessary to carry it out. It is equally important that every church, as far as possible, should have a group of people who meet together regularly for prayer and fellowship and so provide help for newly committed Christians to grow in the faith.

The third case of severe demonisation that came my way concerned a young man who came to me for help. I was asked by someone to pray with him. As we sat chatting together I had no idea that there was anything seriously wrong. He seemed to be a normal young man about twenty years of age going through a time of disappointment or depression. I do recall that he seemed to be very unhappy. As any other Christian minister would have done, I finished our time together with prayer. It was one of those occasions when I knew that I was "praying in the Spirit" (Ephesians 6.18) or praying according to "the mind of the Spirit" (Romans 8.26, 27). When I asked the young man how he felt about things, expecting him to say he was much better, his reply was very definite. He was much worse! I called my wife, who was waiting for me in the next room, to come and assist. I sensed that there was something sinister here. As soon as we began to pray and minister to him, a strange thing happened. He slithered off the chair and on to the floor where he hissed and wriggled like a snake and crawled face down under various pieces of furniture in the room, attempting to hide. I pulled him out into the open by his legs several times. Eventually, we got him to his feet and arranged for him to come back for another session.

When he came back, I had assembled a small team with a view to performing an exorcism. The symptoms suggested that a demon was present and a major exorcism required. I am sorry to say that we did not succeed. The snake like movements continued and in response to my commands to the demon to let go and come out, there was a small voice that said quietly, "I am not going. He belongs to me. I am staying."

In retrospect, I have to ask myself, Was this a genuine case of demonic activity? Why did we not succeed? Were there drugs involved? Was he acting? Was this a case of Multiple Personality Disorder (MPD)? The truth is I do not know. What I do know is, that he left home next day and travelled to another part of the United Kingdom without saying to anyone where he was going. I invited his parents to come and see me and told them what had happened. They did not appear to be surprised and made no comment. These cases in which demons manifest themselves arguing or resisting or threatening, require major exorcism.

At this point I need to move away a little from personal experience and pass on some important guidelines that I have discovered here and there from general reading, conferences and discussion on the subject. There are rules that need to be followed if we are to avoid serious mistakes. It would be very easy to get into situations that cause acute embarrassment or lead to more serious consequences.

My mind goes back to an attempted exorcism in Barnsley some years ago. After an all night attempt at exorcism a man called Michael Taylor went home and murdered his wife. It was an appalling tragedy. Major exorcism is a serious business and needs to be exercised with extreme care.

Those who are called to minister to someone who is severely or moderately demonised should ensure that they have a back-up team of mature Christians who will pray and some of whom will be present at the exorcism. In the case of very severe demonisation which is rare in this country, it is desirable if possible to have a doctor or psychiatrist in attendance. The patient should be carefully assessed beforehand by the team to ensure that exorcism is appropriate and necessary. Under no circumstances should anyone attempt an exorcism alone. The patient should be treated with the utmost compassion and respect. Those who have come to minister are not fighting the patient but the demons who are controlling him. Things may take on the atmosphere of a battle but the battle is not against the patient. It is against demons from hell.

I know of a case where a group of enthusiastic, immature Christians tried to carry out an exorcism of a girl in England. The girl is well known to me. She suffers from an acute form of hormonal imbalance which affects her moods and behaviour. I have visited her in a psychiatric hospital on occasions. When she was young she went to England and joined a small group of enthusiastic Christians whose ardour was not matched by their wisdom. The girl's behaviour and moods led them to believe that she had a demon and they set about getting rid of it. They became more and more agitated and aggressive as they made no headway. In their determination and excitement, they held the girl on the floor and pushed a bible into her mouth, so that she could hardly breathe.

That is not Christian exorcism. It is a form of abuse against a girl who was mentally and emotionally disturbed. Sadly, it is not the only occasion that I have heard about someone who needed help but was psychologically or physically or emotionally abused in a so called exorcism. Perhaps the most important rule of all in attempting a major exorcism is to use sanctified common sense and to remember that you are trying to help, comfort and bring peace to someone in great distress. If the Lord Jesus Christ has given authority to his Church to cast out demons, there is no need to shout or use force. All that is necessary is to exercise that authority by giving the word of command firmly in his Name and to go on repeating it with confidence until the deed is done and the mission is accomplished. Again it is my considered opinion that this work of major exorcism should only be attempted by those called, trained and authorized by the Church for this work.

The Christian's Authority

It is important to know that we have the authority and power of JesusChrist to cast out demons. Several texts of scripture could be quoted but I will refer to only one which speaks to me with great affirmation and assurance. I invite all Christian leaders to receive it as a precious promise from the Lord to his Church.

> "I have given you authority to trample on snakes and scorpions and over all the power of the enemy: nothing will harm you."
> (Luke 10.19)

I find Michael Harper's comments on the passage containing this text very interesting and helpful. It's about the sending out of the seventy into the towns of Galilee to prepare the people for Jesus' coming. Jesus gave them authority to heal the sick (Luke 10.9). He did not say anything about casting out demons as he had done when commissioning the twelve apostles (Luke 9.1). Michael Harper writes as follows:

> "When Jesus sent the seventy on ahead of him his commission to them was somewhat different from that of the twelve. They were told to heal the sick, but there was no mention of power and authority over "all demons" which he had specifically delegated to the Twelve. The seventy, however, exceeded themselves and even their commission, for they made the discovery that "even the demons are subject to us in your name!" Jesus did not rebuke them for going beyond their orders. But he cautioned them against the sin of pride. The source of a Christian's joy should be in his status, not his success."

Our Lord's words are clear:

> "Do not rejoice that the spirits submit to you, but rejoice that your names are written in heaven." (Luke 10.20)

It is obvious that Jesus regarded this report from the seventy as a new and important development in the work of the kingdom that he had come to establish. He did not receive it casually or play it down. Nowhere in the gospels do we read of Jesus rejoicing with greater fervour. The picture that Luke is painting is that of a man ecstatic, celebrating with uplifted hands and great joy.

> "At that time Jesus, full of joy through the Holy Spirit, said: "I praise you, father, Lord of heaven and earth, because you have hidden these

things from the wise and learned, and revealed them to little children. Yes, father, for this was your good pleasure." (Luke 10.21).

The whole subject of demonology has been studied at some depth over the centuries and many books have been written. That is something for which we should be grateful. It is right that those with the ability should apply themselves to the examination of a subject that has such a prominent place in the ministry and teaching of Jesus. However, that is not a necessary qualification for exercising this ministry. Jesus spoke about the Father hiding these things from the wise and learned and revealing them to little children. The Lord is pleased to use those who are childlike in faith, dedication and obedience.

Four Stages in Exorcism

1 – Repentance

The literal meaning of repentance is a change of mind. That may be difficult, if not impossible, for a severely demonised person. By definition such a person is, in varying degrees, under the control of an alien being. A willingness to change his mind and so be changed in heart and life, may be the one thing he cannot do. We may need to counsel a distressed person to show that true repentance is a gift from God. He gives it to us if we are ready and willing to receive.

In the Anglican Book of Common Prayer, the absolution at Morning Prayer exhorts, "Wherefore, let us beseech Him to grant us true repentance and his Holy Spirit." We find the same thought in the Acts of the Apostles. "God exalted Jesus to his own right hand as Prince and Saviour that he might give repentance and forgiveness of sin to Israel." (Acts 5.31)

So the question that needs to be asked when repentance is difficult is: Do you want this change of mind that the Bible calls repentance? Are you prepared to ask God to give it to you? If there is an unwillingness within, are you willing to be made willing?

Alice (Part 1 Chapter 2) was not willing to repent. She was not willing to be made willing, so the exorcism had to be aborted. No one can be set free from evil if he is not willing to be set free.

2 – Binding and Loosing

Here is something that most Christian leaders tend to ignore. The business of binding and loosing is clearly included in the teaching of Jesus. What does it mean?

Let's look at two references to binding and loosing in the gospels.

The first is in the context of the healing of a demonised man who was blind and mute. (Matthew 12.22-29) Obviously, the Pharisees saw this healing as a casting out of demons. They reacted with these words:

> "It is only by Beelzebub, the prince of demons, that this fellow casts out demons."

Jesus saw their comment as illogical and ridiculous.

> "If Satan drives out Satan, he is divided against himself. How then can his kingdom stand?"

Then follows Jesus' teaching about binding.

> "How can anyone enter a strong man's house and carry off his possessions unless he first ties up the strong man? Then he can rob his house."

What is Jesus saying here? Is he not saying that Satan is bound under his authority and power? Is he not claiming that his casting out of demons is a demonstration that he has first overpowered and bound the strong man? How could he enter Satan's house and steal his goods, if he did not first tie up the owner? Every time a person is rescued from the dominion of Satan, Satan is bound by the authority and power of Jesus Christ. "All authority and power is given to me" said Jesus, "therefore go and make disciples...and surely I am with you always." The power to bind and loose has been given to the Church.

There are two other references to binding and loosing in S. Matthew's Gospel.

(a) The first of these texts is obviously addressed to Peter. It was Peter who declared: "You are the Christ, the Son of the living God." In reply, Jesus states:

> "You are Peter, and on this rock I will build my church, and the gates of Hades will not overcome it. I will give you the keys of the kingdom of heaven; whatever you bind on earth will be bound in heaven, and whatever you loose on earth will be loosed in heaven." (Matthew 16.18,19)

In the Greek text the "you" is singular because it is addressed to Peter.

(b) The second text is addressed to a local church and this time the "you" is plural. It is important to consider it in the full context.

"If your brother sins against you, go and show him his fault, just between the two of you. If he listens to you, you have won your brother over. But if he will not listen, take one or two others along, so that every matter may be established by the testimony of two or three witnesses. If he refuses to listen to them, tell it to the Church; and if he refuses to listen even to the Church, treat him as you would a pagan or a tax collector. I tell you the truth, whatever you bind on earth will be bound in heaven, and whatever you loose on earth will be loosed in heaven." (Matthew 18,15-18)

A controversy about the true interpretation of our Lord's words concerning "binding and loosing" has raged across the centuries. Many scholars have commented, giving different explanations. Michael Harper makes the following useful, common sense observation:

"The trouble with this verse (Matthew 16.19) is that so many Protestants have spent their energies seeking to prove that this does not refer to the Pope, or to priestly absolution, that they have largely neglected to find out what it does refer to! Likewise Roman Catholics have so ardently defended their position, that they too seem to have restricted and misapplied it. Surely amongst other things it is another reference to our authority to bind evil powers in Jesus' name and to loose those who are subjected to bondage." (Spiritual Warfare, page 115)

Exercising Authority

The right time for this binding to take place may be before or after the patient's repentance. After a time of talking with him or her about the need to repent of sin and reject all that is evil, it may become clear that there is severe interference from the demon. That can take many forms such as fear, argument, awkwardness, nastiness, stubbornness, inability to repent, anger, loss of speech and so on. Every device imaginable may be used to hinder progress. That is the time to exercise the authority that the Lord gives to his Church to bind and to loose.

"You foul and evil spirit, in the name of Jesus Christ and in accordance with the authority that he has given to his Church, I bind you and I forbid you to speak or interfere with this man/woman. I take away your power to influence or restrict him (or her) in any way. I loose you

(John/Mary) from bondage. You are now free to repent of your sins and to cooperate with us as we seek to lead you to total and permanent freedom as a child of God indwelt by the Holy Spirit."

Sometimes the binding may take place after repentance and before you make the final onslaught and cast it out. By so doing you weaken its power to resist and the event takes place without a fight or a scene. There is no reason that there should be a fuss when the time comes for casting out a spirit. It may happen with a scream or a whimper or the patient falling down. In minor cases it will happen in silence and without any observable reaction except tears of relief, joy and peace.

It is important to grasp fully that you are exercising the authority of Jesus Christ. It's your job to speak in his name "I bind you...I take you captive...I strip you of all power to resist...You are weak and helpless in my hands and you must obey...I speak in his name and by the power of the Holy Spirit..."

3 – Word of Command

Having the cooperation of the patient and having bound the spirit, the next step is to speak the word of command. The Lord has given authority to his Church to cast out demons. This is not done by making a polite request for the spirit to leave. The command should be issued firmly with determination and authority.

"You foul spirit, I am speaking to you now in the name and with the authority of Jesus Christ. At my command you will depart from this person whom you have tormented for many days and you will go to your own place. I have bound you and stripped you of your power to resist. You will go quietly and you will hurt no one as you leave. Go now to that place that the Lord Jesus Christ appoints for you and there you will remain till he releases you."

In a case of severe demonization which is very rare in this country, you may experience resistance. Continue to issue the command.

There is a suggestion in the story of the Gadarene demoniac that Jesus pressurised the demons by *continuing* to issue a command to leave. It is as if the demon was resisting. (Mark 5.8 may be translated: "For Jesus *was saying* to him 'Come out...'" The verb in Greek is in the imperfect tense). Demons can and will resist. You may have to go on issuing the command. There may come a time when you realise that you are not going to succeed. In that case it is wiser to stop and try another time. It may become clear later, why the demon was able to resist your commands.

Warning

The case of someone who is severely or moderately demonized should not be tackled by immature, untrained or inexperienced people. I believe that it's a job for those who have been authorised as leaders of their Church and preferably ordained. This is not a job for freelancers of which there are many in Christian circles today. People who find themselves attracted to the sensational in Christian ministry, should seriously examine their motives before rushing into this work. It is not for those who are young or immature in mind and heart. It should be approached with reluctance but with a willingness to obey; with reluctance because it is an ugly and dangerous business; with obedience because the Lord has called us to do it; and with compassion because someone needs help. The three words that should always be uppermost in this ministry are reluctance, obedience and compassion. The absence of *any* of these conditions is an indication that we should examine our motives carefully.

4 – Follow-Up

The Lord's teaching is very clear. It is not enough to cast out demons and leave it there. Jesus taught that demons can return.

> "When an evil spirit comes out of a man, it goes through arid places seeking rest and does not find it. Then it says, 'I will return to the house I left!' When it arrives, it finds the house swept clean and put in order. Then it goes and takes seven other spirits more wicked than itself, and they go in and live there. And the final state of that man is worse than the first." (Luke 11.24-26)

The emptiness created by the departure of demons needs to be filled. It is, therefore, essential that the person who has been rid of spirits should put his life in the care of Jesus Christ and be indwelt by the Holy Spirit. I have heard of someone very experienced in the Ministry of Deliverance who would not begin an exorcism of anyone, unless he believed that it would be followed by an act of faith in Jesus Christ. That, he believes, would make things worse. According to the teaching of Jesus, he would be right!

What I have written in this chapter will be of little more than academic interest to those who read. The chances of encountering someone in this country who requires major exorcism are remote. That is not to say that such people do not exist. The more probable situation is that they do exist in larger numbers than we think but are not likely to seek the ministry of the Church.

Chapter Five
Follow-Up

It is essential to keep in mind, when we get involved in the Ministry of Deliverance (or , indeed, in any other aspect of the healing ministry) what our ultimate aim is. It is not just an attempt to rid someone of disease or affliction. Unfortunately, that is how it is usually perceived.

Of course there is always that element in it. When someone seeks help through the ministry of the Church, he does so in the hope that that which is spoiling his life will be removed. Those who attend healing ministry Services do so because they are seeking relief from disease, pain, sickness, depression or some other affliction. They want to get rid of something.

Whilst that is a natural thing to do, and there are many such examples in the healings of Jesus, we should not overlook the positive side. We come to receive health and to be what we believe the Lord wants us to be. This concept is foremost in the aim of the medical profession. A doctor aims to treat the person and not the disease. In the same way, the Church's ministry is directed towards the individual for restoration to health.

This thought will help us to avoid a common mistake when we are trying to exercise the ministry of deliverance. Our aim is not only to set a person free of a spirit which is tormenting him or marring his life. It is to bring him into a relationship with God through Jesus Christ so that he will be fulfilled, walk in peace and find God's purpose for his life.

At some point, the authority that Jesus has given to his Church will be exercised, the spirit will be bound, its power will be broken, and a command will be issued and a man or woman will be set free. However, we need to be aware of the teaching of Jesus that the spirit can and may return. (Matthew 12.43, 44). Sometimes it will prove more difficult to prevent the return of the spirit than to cast it out. That is why a follow up is so important.

In Part 2 Chapter 4, reference is made to the need to lead a demonised person to an act of repentance and faith in Jesus Christ. Unless that is done before, during or after the carrying out of the exorcism, there will not be a lasting change in the person's condition. He will revert to his old ways. There needs to be ongoing and continuous acts of repentance, faith and receiving of the

Holy Spirit. That should not surprise anyone for it is part of every Christian's walk through life.

An illustration from the medical field should make that clear. If a person is suffering from tuberculosis, doctors will administer the treatment necessary to rid the patient of the bacilli that is causing the disease. He will be prescribed drugs to fight the infection and ordered to rest. Advice will be given about his life style in the future and if he follows the rules, he will recover in time. However, if he goes back to his old ways and abuses his body by doing what he has been told not to do, the chances are that the tuberculosis will return. The follow up plan prescribed by the doctors must be observed if restoration to health is going to continue.

The need for cooperation from everyone who wants relief of oppression from evil spirits is paramount. A dentist cannot remove a troublesome tooth from a patient unless he is prepared to sit in the dentist's chair and open his mouth. Cooperation is essential but there the analogy breaks down. The minister needs more from his patient than sitting in his chair. He needs a willingness on the patient's part to repent of his sin, to trust in Jesus as Saviour and Lord and to receive the Holy Spirit as counsellor, companion and friend.

The emphasis in the follow up to deliverance is about these three requirements so that the change wrought in the person's life continues and grows.

First, there is a need for ongoing repentance.

Repentance means more than being sorry for our sins. It means turning from them and adopting a different life style. As the late Most Reverend Donald Coggan, a former Archbishop of Canterbury, described it: "A change of mind resulting in a change of heart and a change of life."

Peter Horrobin, in his book "Healing through Deliverance" writes repeatedly about the possibility of giving to spirits "the legal right" to attach themselves to our lives. That legal right, he writes, we can give by living wilfully sinful lives. There is a constant and continuous need to repent of that which is rebellion against God and contrary to his will. If that proves too difficult and beyond our reach, then in the words of the Absolution in the Anglican Book of Common Prayer: "Let us beseech Him to grant us true repentance and his Holy Spirit."

Second, there is a need for ongoing faith and obedience.

The person who wants to remain spiritually healthy and free from spiritual oppression needs to be constantly renewing and nourishing his faith. That faith should be clear and definite. Saving faith is not mere intellectual assent to certain theological propositions. It is the faith that grows into a personal relationship with God through Jesus Christ. It is the faith that inspired S. Paul to write: "I want to know Christ and the power of his resurrection." (Philippians 3.10) Such faith is the Christian safeguard against the forces of darkness. "Whoever follows me will never walk in darkness." said Jesus. (John 8.12) If the Lord is in control of a person's life, there will not be a domination by evil entities in that life.

Of course, temptations will come. None can escape that. The Lord Jesus himself was "tempted in every way just as we are - yet was without sin." (Hebrews 4.15) The temptations of Jesus continued to the end. "When the devil had finished all this tempting, he left him until an opportune time." (Luke 4.13) We must not expect that it will be different for us. We should remind ourselves constantly of a truth that the devil would seek to hide from us - it is not a sin to be tempted. As the old fashioned hymn puts it: "Yield not to temptation for yielding is sin."

The saying is true: we cannot stop swallows flying over our heads but we can stop them building their nests in our hair.

Third, there is a need for the ongoing fellowship of the Holy Spirit. Every Christian needs that. The many renewals of the Church that have taken place across the centuries have brought to light some aspect of the faith that has been overlooked or neglected. The Charismatic Renewal Movement of the last quarter of the 20th century has laid emphasis on the presence and power of the Holy Spirit in the life of the Christian and of the Church.

Canon John Stott wrote a book in 1958 called: "Your Confirmation". On page 68 he writes: "The Holy Spirit has sometimes been described as the neglected Person of the Trinity." I suspect he would not write that today. Even those who have not been involved in the Charismatic Renewal have been influenced by it and have become more conscious of the activity of the Spirit. The Holy Spirit has moved once more into the centre of the Church's life and teaching which is where he ought to be.

It's amazing to reflect that the Spirit could ever have been neglected in the Church. Week by week we were taught to say: "I believe in the Holy Spirit". He was not excluded from the Church's formularies or liturgy. He was not neglected in the New Testament. Indeed the opposite was the case. He would take the place of Jesus amongst the disciples after the Lord was taken from them. "I will ask the Father, and he will give you another counsellor to be with you for ever, even the Spirit of truth." (John 14.16,17) The Holy Spirit would be with them and in them. (John 14.17) The Holy Spirit would be their teacher. He "will teach you all things and will remind you of everything that I have said to you." (John 14.26)

What would the Holy Spirit do for them? He would give them power. (Acts 1.8) He would mould and shape the disciples, making them like "little Christs", using the expression of C.S. Lewis. The Holy Spirit would change them and make them like their Lord. (Galatians 5.22) The Holy Spirit would affirm them as children of God. (Romans 8.15,16) An essential element in the Church and every Christian life is the gracious presence and power of the Holy Spirit. Repentance and faith should be followed by receiving the Holy Spirit.

Paul asked some disciples at Ephesus: "Did you receive the Holy Spirit when you believed?" (Acts 19.2) For him, the receiving of the Spirit was the sine qua non of belonging to Christ. "If anyone does not have the Spirit of Christ he does not belong to him." (Romans 8.9) How important it is for every follower of Jesus Christ (and especially those who have experienced deliverance from evil influence) to be possessed by the Holy Spirit. Without that he is vulnerable when attack comes.

Jesus issued a warning about leaving a house unguarded and empty.

> "When an evil spirit comes out of a man, it goes through arid places seeking rest and does not find it. Then it says I will return to the house I left. When it arrives, it finds the house swept clean and in order. Then it goes and takes with it seven other spirits more wicked than itself and they go in and live there and the final condition of that man is worse than the first." (Luke 11.24-26)

These three acts of ongoing repentance, ongoing faith in Jesus and ongoing receiving of the Spirit are an absolutely essential part of the follow up required to the ministry of deliverance, whether it be major or minor or somewhere in between.

Pastoral Care

The three ongoing acts outlined above are important general principles but more is required.

A person who has found new life in Christ needs to be nourished and fed like a new born babe until he has grown strong in the faith. He cannot be left to fend for himself. He needs special attention and especially so if he has experienced a deliverance from forces and habits that were destroying his life. That's why it is so important that the leaders of the Church need to be aware of the ministry of deliverance. They need to learn more about it. It is not enough to call in the so called expert and leave it to him to get on with it. Someone called in may be helpful in dealing with the problem in the initial stages but the follow up is in the hands of the local priest or minister. I have seen valuable opportunities for evangelism wasted because someone has taken the attitude that this sort of ministry is outside his knowledge and experience. The follow up to the ministry of deliverance is little different to the follow up required in other forms of ministry in the Church.

What is needed?

In everyday terms, what is required after this ministry is a matter of common sense. They are the things that any ordinary, caring person will give, such as understanding, sympathy, interest, encouragement, a non-judgemental attitude, practical help.

Of course more is required, namely those things that every pastor and congregation is called to provide. They are so obvious that they may be overlooked or neglected. I will refer to some of them briefly. They are fundamental in every Christian life and particularly important when seeking to build up and strengthen someone who has been set free from spiritual oppression.

Prayer

Obviously, prayer is important. Those of us who have been praying for as long as we can remember may not fully realise the need to learn to pray. Jesus taught his disciples to pray. Indeed, as they watched him pray they asked him specifically: "Lord teach us to pray." Prayer is a native tendency of the human soul but man needs to be taught before he progresses towards the heights reached by the great saints and mystics of the past.

How many churches have occasional teaching courses on prayer? The Reverend Brother David Jardine of the Society of S. Francis in Belfast has produced a number of excellent booklets and leaflets on the subject which would prove valuable to those who want to pursue the subject further. Moreover he provides teaching sessions on prayer which would be of tremendous help to those who want to learn how to pray. He is always willing to make himself available in preaching and teaching when invited.

Holy Scripture

Linked with prayer is the reading of Holy Scripture. No Christian of any standing can grow strong in the faith unless he applies himself to the study of Christian teaching as recorded in the New Testament. As every Church leader knows, many helps are available to guide his people in the private study of the Bible. Added to that, there is the precious opportunity that clergy have every week to expound God's truth to a congregation gathered together "to hear and receive God's Holy Word." (Book of Common Prayer)

Holy Communion

Coupled with learning to pray and receiving God's word is the celebration of Christ's victory over all the power of the enemy at a Communion Service. There is the opportunity to share in that victory at every Eucharist. Nothing can be more important for the man or woman set free from the forces of darkness, than the receiving of the body and blood of Christ in the Holy Communion. "Our souls are strengthened and refreshed by the body and blood of Christ as our bodies are by the bread and wine." (Church Catechism B.C.P.)

Prayer, Scripture, Eucharist - these are the foundation pillars on which the follow up to the ministry of deliverance is built. One other pillar needs to be mentioned. I refer to fellowship, that great New Testament word specially coined to describe the concern that the first disciples of Christ had for one another.

Christian Fellowship

Obviously, the ideal situation in a church is that fellowship should include the whole congregation. In one sense it does, for the Church is the Body of Christ and all baptised believers are members of it. On the other hand, in a large congregation that fellowship may not be manifest because people do not know one another, have no conscious relationship with one another or are not close to one another. That's why it is very important that every congregation has within it groups of people who meet together on a regular basis to pray, study and encourage one another in living out the faith in daily life. Such groups are invaluable in establishing and strengthening a recent convert in the faith. Without such fellowship it is difficult to see how a follow- up to the ministry of deliverance can be sustained.

The importance of fellowship in every congregation cannot be over emphasised. Notice how often the expression "one another" occurs in the New

Testament: "love one another, be kind to one another, bear one another's burdens, encourage one another, pray for one another, build one another up ..." These are only a few quotes that come readily to mind. There are many more. It would be a useful and profitable exercise to look them up in a concordance. They are the basis of the ministry of follow-up to all who need help in the struggle of life.

Chapter Six

Exorcising Places

Over the years, I have been invited to minister in places (including homes, shops and hospitals) where people have been convinced of an unwelcome spirit presence. Of course I cannot prove that there was objective reality in every case. Sceptics will always be able to explain it away. How can I be sure of the cause of the disturbance? How can I prove that the activity described to me is caused by a spirit? The truth is I cannot. All that I can be sure about is that the people who have asked me to come are genuine, frightened and in need of spiritual help and comfort. They are convinced that what they have heard and seen and experienced is the result of paranormal activity. In the great majority of cases, I have had no reason to believe that they were mistaken.

If someone tells you that at some time during a service of worship, God spoke to their heart and as a result, their life has been changed, how do you react? Do you doubt their word? Do you say that they are very impressionable? Do you have serious doubts about what they are saying? Are you inclined to disbelieve them? Of course not.

Suppose that same person asked you to call at his home and tells you that he believes there is a spirit active there and gives you an account of many strange things that are happening, what do you do? Do you believe him? Do you put it all down to imagination? Do you think to yourself "this is psychological"? It depends on the kind of person with whom you are dealing. If you would normally pay heed to what he says, you are bound to listen sympathetically to what he is saying now. You cannot believe him at one level and disbelieve him at another.

The most important principle to be observed in all these cases is to listen sympathetically. You can be sure that the person who is opening his heart to you is not finding it easy. He has had to overcome the fear that you will think that he is very silly and unbelievably gullible. So put him at his ease by listening to him sympathetically.

Of course you will look for a natural cause. Every house has its own noises - water running through pipes, wind in the chimney or the rafters, rats or mice scurrying about, faulty wires causing the lights to flicker, catches on doors allowing the doors to be blown open, someone playing tricks and secretly moving objects from one place to another. There are plenty of natural causes that need to be investigated and eliminated before concluding that some action is required.

I had a case where a young mother was very disturbed because she could hear faint voices in the next room and a child crying. Usually she would hear these things in the middle of the night and on rising to attend her baby would find him deeply asleep. I was asked to see her and found her very upset. I listened to her story. Could these voices be coming from next door? No, there were no children next door on either side. I was shown round the house and spotted a baby monitor. A baby monitor is a modern device of two parts - a microphone and a receiver. The microphone is left in the baby's room and the receiver with the parents, so that the child's movements and noises can be heard by the parents in another room. I knew from experience that this device could pick up noises from another house. That's exactly what was happening. It was a mother consoling her crying baby in the night. That ghost was laid without an exorcism.

It is difficult to find words to describe exactly what is taking place in a home where there is paranormal activity. A spirit may manifest its presence in all kinds of ways. I have given various examples in chapter 11. Each of these stories that I am telling would have no value at all, if I were not writing out of personal experience. I am sharing them with others as others shared them with me. I believe they are true. I am convinced that, by the power of the Spirit, and in the name of Jesus Christ, places have been set free. They have been set free by the power of Christian ministry from what I choose to call a disturbing presence. The disturbing presence may be benign and harmless, or evil and destructive.

One of the problems that faces those who are called to "exorcise" places is trying to decide what kind of spirit is present and active. Dr Kenneth McAll writes about earth-bound spirits and the unquiet dead. In his book "Healing the Family Tree" he gives many examples from his own experience. One has to decide for oneself if such teaching rings true. Certainly, I have encountered cases where it would appear that there is the presence of an earth-bound spirit, that is, the spirit of a departed person who, for some reason that I cannot explain, has got "stuck" and has not been able to let go of the old life and go on to the next stage on the journey.

One of the first "haunted" houses that I was asked to visit was in the Stranmillis area of Belfast. The house was occupied by three or four university students. When I arrived they were terrified and all sleeping together in one room. They had all heard strange knockings and footsteps from time to time. Things came to a climax when two of the girls wakened in the middle of the night and saw a man standing at the foot of their bed. They described him to me in some detail. They said he was grey-haired and wearing a tradesman's brown overalls, the apparel often worn in Belfast by factory workers in earlier days. According to the two girls, this apparition stood staring at them with a puzzled look.

If we assume that what the girls described had objective reality, it would seem that this was an earth-bound spirit, one who had lived there and was still attached to this house and for some reason was still around. I have no difficulty in accepting that theory but I would respect those who differ from me. This is a grey area.

There is an interesting sequence to the story. The mother of one of the girls had lived in this same house about thirty years earlier when she was a student. She had not told her daughter about a rumour that had been circulating in those days. Indeed, she had forgotten about it. She remembered that that house was said to be haunted when she was a student.

One theory that is often suggested by Dr McAll and others is that earth-bound spirits (commonly called ghosts) make their presence known to draw attention to themselves in an effort to find help. True or not, it's an interesting theory. If it is true (and I am inclined to believe that it may be) it means that an exorcism or "the laying of a ghost" may be helping both the living and the dead!

I recall another case which illustrates the difficulty of distinguishing between an earth-bound spirit and an evil spirit or demon. I had a parishioner who was very distressed. At that time she was loosely attached to the church where I was Rector. My first encounter with her was in hospital. After that, I visited her in her home and found that the cause of her distress was that her mother had died a few years previously and was appearing to her regularly. A team from the local Pentecostal Church had visited her and told her she had a demon. At the time, I regarded that as nonsense. Eventually, she was taken into a psychiatric hospital but she came out, no better than she was when she went in. Indeed, in some ways she was worse.

A few weeks after she had been released from hospital, I had a visiting clergyman from England, the Rev. Trevor Dearing. He was noted for his healing and exorcism ministry. I persuaded the lady to come to one of his meetings and told Trevor about her. When I described to him how her departed mother kept appearing to her and causing her great distress, without any hesitation, he said to me, "That's not her mother. That's a tormenting spirit impersonating her mother." He called it a "familiar spirit". That was a new idea to me!

I offered to point her out to him when she came forward for prayer but he said that would not be necessary. He would recognise her, and he did! As she stood there before him, he commanded the demon to leave. The lady fell to the ground and lay there for about half an hour. "Leave her" he said, "she will be all right." and he went on ministering to others. After about half an hour we carried the lady into the vestry. By this time her husband was getting very worried. She showed no signs of recovering consciousness. Eventually she did sit up and went home. Her mother never appeared to her again. It was my privilege to present her for confirmation about a year later. What some might believe was an "earth-bound" spirit was a tormenting, impersonating spirit, that should be cast out.

How does a spirit, be it benign or malign, manifest itself? It does so in many different ways, ranging from appearing in human form as an apparition, to conveying to people the "sense" that they are being observed. The way that a spirit does this is beyond explanation. Obviously, there are laws that govern the spirit world that have not been revealed to us. That spirits can and do manifest themselves to certain people is the plain teaching of scripture. There are many examples of that in the Old and New Testaments. We have only to think of the story of the Transfiguration, the appearance of the departed to many in Jerusalem after the crucifixion of Jesus, the spirits who spoke to Jesus through the lips of different men, the spirit that manifested itself to the witch of Endor, the appearance of angels to various people, including the Blessed Virgin Mary. These stories speak to us of spiritual laws that are outside our ken.

The reasons that people are convinced that there is a strange, mysterious and unwanted presence in their home have been, in my experience, many and varied. Examples that have been given to me include the occasional appearance of an elderly woman in one of the bedrooms; the "sensing" by a mature senior civil servant, who lived alone and called himself agnostic, that when he entered his house, there was someone there watching him; strange noises coming from other parts of a house; inexplicable coldness in some places; animals showing frightened behaviour, cowering or trembling; dogs staring at something with fixed gaze and concentrated attention. These are all accounts that have been given to me as I have investigated situations when requested to do so. I have given examples in fuller detail in Part 1 Chapter 6.

Having pondered on these things for many years, I have concluded that such disturbances that occur in certain places, can and should be cleared up through the ministry of the church. If they are caused by earth-bound spirits that have got stuck or tied to some place with which they have been closely associated, they should be released. Dr Kenneth McAll's theory is that they can be released through prayer at a Eucharist. If they are malign spirits, they can be commanded to leave in the same way. For me as one who acts to clear a place from an unwanted presence, it is helpful to be aware that I do not need to know whether a spirit is earth-bound or demonic. It is sufficient to have the wonderful assurance that our Lord Jesus Christ died and descended to Hades, the place of departed spirits, and "preached to the spirits in prison." (1 Peter 3 v.18, 19) Whatever that means, or how it is interpreted, it says to me that the Lord has the knowledge, authority and power to deal with every spirit that has lost its way or entered into a situation where it ought not to be. Jesus said: "All authority in heaven and on earth has been given to me." Whilst we cannot understand or see what is going on in the spirit world, we have the assurance that the Lord knows and understands and is in full control. In his name and by the power of the Holy Spirit, we can exercise effectually his authority and power.

It may be helpful to some church leaders, if I share with them in a simple and straightforward way, how I deal with the situations I have described. There are three elements in my approach.

Sympathetic listening

First, I go to the house of those who ask for help. The primary object of the visit is to bring comfort, faith and hope to the situation. Normally, those who are living there are very frightened people. They may have been going through this trauma for months or years. Their health may be impaired. Probably they have kept this problem to themselves because they think that none will believe them - or worse, people will laugh and dismiss what they say.

When I visit the home, I bring one or two others with me to help me assess the situation and to act as a back-up team. One member of the team takes notes so that, if necessary, we can go back over all that we have been told. The mere act of sitting down with the family and listening sympathetically to their story is, in itself, a real source of comfort and healing for them. When we arrive, there is usually an atmosphere of fear and apprehension, but in less than five minutes, that is gone. The relief is almost tangible.

Proclaiming Christ in the Eucharist

Second, having decided that there is enough evidence of paranormal activity, we prepare to have a Service of Holy Communion. It is usually celebrated at the place where most of the disturbance is focused. Before the Service, I explain to everyone why I am doing what I am doing. I am not performing an act of white magic. Jesus himself gave us this Service to remind us of His death and victory over Satan. He overcame Satan's final and greatest assault against Him on the cross. He demonstrated his power and authority by his resurrection.

Every Eucharist is a proclamation of the death and resurrection of Jesus. Paul writes: "Whenever you eat this bread and drink this cup you proclaim the Lord's death till He come." (1 Corinthians 11.26). Eucharist is a proclamation of the absolute, complete and total victory of Christ over Satan. So, before the Service begins, I pray to the Father to appoint angels to gather to this Eucharist whatever spirit is visiting this place, that I may proclaim before it the victory, authority and power of Jesus Christ.

> "Father, we rejoice in your great love and in the victory of your son Jesus Christ over sin, death and hell. We pray you to send angels to gather to this place any spirits that have been active here, that we may proclaim before them the death of Jesus and the only way to you and all that is prepared for us in heaven, through the same Jesus Christ, our Lord. Amen."

(This prayer may be altered to suit the circumstances.)

It is possible that not everyone will want to receive the Holy Communion, so that should be settled before the Service begins.

Having been "strengthened and refreshed by the Body and Blood of Christ" (Church Catechism, Anglican B.C.P. Page 262) we are now ready to exercise the authority and power of Jesus Christ against whatever spirit is disturbing this place.

Third, the celebrant, or one appointed by him, now addresses the disturbing spirit with these or similar words:

> "Spirit, I address you now in the name, and with the authority of Jesus Christ. I have power to bind you and power to release you. You are (or I command you) to go immediately to the place that Jesus Christ has

appointed for you. I bind you in the name of Jesus and take away all your power to resist. You will go quietly and hurt no one as you go and you will not return to this place again for ever. The angels appointed by God will take you away to your own place and there you will remain under the authority and according to the mercy of Jesus Christ."

After a short pause the celebrant gives praise to God.

"Father we thank you that this spirit (or these spirits) are leaving and going to where you want them to be. We ask you to cleanse this house from all defilement, that it may become, for those who dwell here, a house of peace. Send your angels to guard this house and protect those who dwell here. Unite them in love and draw them to yourself that they may rejoice in you as their Saviour and Lord for ever. Amen"

The celebrant will now walk round the house, led by a member of the household, saying an appropriate short prayer of dedication and blessing in each room. Returning to the others who will be praying at the place of the celebration of the Eucharist, the service will be concluded with the Lord's Prayer, a prayer of thanksgiving and the Blessing.

Suitable Collects and Readings

The Church of Ireland Alternative Prayerbook:

Collects:
Lent 2, Lent 5, Easter Eve, Easter 5, Pentecost 9.

Epistles:
Ephesians 6.10-18; 2 Corinthians 5.6-10; 1 John 4.1-3;

Gospels:
Luke 10.v17-20; Luke 23.33, 39-43; John 6.35-40. Revelation 1.12-18

Whilst the Order of Service or the choice of Collects and Readings will not hinder or reduce the efficacy of this ministry, obviously the choice will be governed by your assessment of the situation. Are you dealing with a malign or destructive spirit, or does it seem more likely that it is an earth-bound spirit?

There is no need to shout or get excited when speaking the word of command to a spirit, but the exorcist should speak in a firm tone, exhibiting plainly that he is speaking with authority and expects his orders to be obeyed. An exorcist does not make requests. He commands. Spirits are not likely to obey anyone who speaks with uncertain or hesitating voice. A Christian exorcist speaks in the name of the King of kings and Lord of lords - the ultimate and final authority in heaven and on earth.

As an Anglican, I have written from an Anglican perspective. Of course, Christians of other denominations will follow their own ritual for celebrating the Holy Communion.

The important thing is to give the Lord all the glory when the exorcism has been successfully accomplished. "Deliver us from evil. Yours is the kingdom, the power and the glory."

After the service it is appropriate to sing a hymn as was done at that first Eucharist.

Chapter Seven
Exorcising Poltergeists?

Poltergeist activity in its strict sense will not be subdued or stopped by an exorcism. It is not caused by the presence of a spirit. That is the conclusion of the Anglican Bishop of Exeter Study Group on exorcism. Nevertheless it is possible, in my opinion, that spirit activity can be linked with poltergeist activity (See Part 1, Chapters 5 and 6).

It is important that those involved in the caring professions (particularly priests, ministers and pastors) should know what to do or how to help those who are perturbed or frightened by poltergeist activity. In its more severe form it can be a terrifying experience. (The events described in Chapter 1 or Part 1 concerning poltergeist activity at Coonian and Derrygonnelly in Co Fermanagh are good examples).

What should a local priest, pastor or minister do when called to help? How should he proceed? The following steps should be taken with the aim of restoring peace and tranquillity to the home.

1. Respond to a call for help as soon as possible. The family will be suffering acute distress if the disturbance is severe.

2. Sit down with the family and show understanding and concern about what is happening.

3. Put the family at ease by spending time with them and encouraging them to talk about what they have heard or seen or experienced.

4. Do not show any sign that you are dubious or sceptical about what they are saying. Most people are hesitant about sharing these things with others in case they will be thought foolish or naive.

5. Of course you will be asking yourself questions and looking for natural causes of the events described. Could the noises be coming from waterpipes or radiators or the chimney or next door?

6. Try to share what you know about poltergeist activity. (See Chapter 5 Part 1). When it is explained, that will relieve the terror and bring comfort.

Once you have come to the conclusion that there is, or seems to be, genuine poltergeist activity, the next step is to search in your mind for the "owner." Consider the various members of the household. Make enquiries and try to ask leading questions about the young people. Are any going through anxiety or strain? You will be praying for the guidance of the Holy Spirit that he will show you the likely person.

In my experience it is not difficult to find the "owner." Once you think you know who he or she is, talk to the parents alone and explain what you have learned about poltergeists. It would not be wise or kind to explain to any young person that he or she is the epicentre of the disturbance and "owner" of the so called poltergeist. Avoid that.

Pray with the family together, and then ask permission to talk to the young people in turn. That way you can counsel the over-wrought child and minister to him or her spiritually seeking to bring healing and comfort. You will probably need to do that often, until things quieten down.

I believe that most families will respond favourably, if you show you are not shocked or afraid of what is going on. The assurance that the disturbance is not caused by a demon, spirit or ghost, that it is a nuisance but will not cause personal harm, that it will gradually cease over a few weeks and peace will return, brings great comfort. The advice given by someone, that the best way to treat a poltergeist is to regard it as a family pet, sounds flippant and facetious but it may not be a bad way to proceed.

A paper produced by the Christian Exorcism Study Group makes the following observation:

> "If the nature of the poltergeist is explained, those suffering from its activities will be able to treat it with the affectionate contempt it deserves and a rapid fade-out will result. Where appropriate, a solemn blessing of the premises will help. Where family tensions are discovered, the blessing of the family as a unit may also take place. The performing of exorcism and other religious rites alone is quite ineffective in removing true poltergeist phenomena. Indeed, it can make matters worse. Counselling may in most cases be very effective and all that is required."

Returning to the case I have described near Randalstown, (Chapter 5 Part 1) I carried out the steps outlined above. It was obvious to me that Rosemary, the 15 year old girl, was the one at the centre of the paranormal activity. I sensed her unhappiness from the beginning, although she was not present during our conversations. It seemed that she absented herself deliberately. I was aware of the tension and sensed that she was not happy with her circumstances. Relationships were sour. She found it difficult to accept her situation and stay in the home. I talked with her alone and while she voiced no complaint I picked up the "vibes". A few days after our second visit to the home, she left and went to live in North Antrim. The poltergeist activity ceased immediately.

An Interesting Case

About 1994 I was asked by my Bishop to investigate paranormal activity in an old people's home in Co. Antrim. It proved to be an interesting case in that it had all the hallmarks of poltergeist activity, from the knockings which were not excessively loud, contents of cupboards strewn about the floor, lights turned off and on repeatedly, buzzers going off in the middle of the night, but all the patients fast asleep when attended!

To verify what we were being told and to confirm its accuracy, one of the doctors who looked after the home, was called. He came and substantiated the truth of the account we were given.

One very unusual happening was the undressing of one of the residents. The lady was very old and handicapped and totally incapable of doing anything for herself. She had to be dressed and undressed by a member of staff. She was not able to move or get out of bed. When her helper arrived to perform her daily task of washing and feeding her, she found to her amazement that the lady's nightdress had been taken off in the night and was lying on the floor.

Another unusual feature was the sighting of what was described by all the members of staff as "a black figure." It was seen in different parts of the house. The lady who owned the house and ran the home for aged residents showed me round and pointed to a recess in one of the corridor walls where she had seen the black figure. I must admit that that was an eerie experience for me and must have been even more so for her. Small wonder that one of the members of staff had a nervous breakdown!

Perhaps the most bizarre event that took place was what happened when two members of staff went to a large linen walk-in cupboard. When one of them opened the door, the black figure jumped out and she felt herself being pushed up against the opposite wall in a state of total shock. It took place so quickly that she could do nothing but scream. The other member of staff, who was following her, saw it happen and fled. She saw her friend "lifted off the ground about two feet high" (her words) and then pushed against the wall behind her.

When the cupboard was examined later the linen was found in a state of total disorder.

Most of the sightings were by members of staff but the lady who had been undressed mysteriously, complained. She was frightened by a strange person who "turned her round in the bed." Of course, the residents were not told anything of what was going on.

I arranged two visits to the home. On the first, I was able to bring with me four or five clergy. The Bishop of Connor had called his clergy to a pre-Lenten retreat not far away and on a free afternoon we travelled to the home in two cars. We sat down with six or seven members of staff and heard their story. I suggested that this seemed to be poltergeist activity and explained briefly to those present the cause of what was happening, as I understood it, and that it was necessary to find the epicentre or "owner." That was not easy in an old people's home where many of the residents were bed-ridden. The members of staff could think of only one resident who was very awkward and difficult, so I went to see her and found her amiable enough and appreciative of the ministry of prayer for her and all the other residents. I was not convinced that the disturbance sprang from her or that she was the cause. When I returned to the group we chatted for a while, prayed for God's protection and blessing for the staff and those for whom they cared and left. It was obvious that the visit of several clergy and the assurance we were able to give, brought great comfort to a very concerned and frightened group of people.

However, a second visit was necessary. After I contacted the lady owner of the house I heard that things were no better and, indeed, may have got worse.

I was puzzled by the constant appearance of the black figure. Was this pure poltergeist activity or was there a presence of something else in the midst of it all? I knew from experience in cases of earth-bound or demonic spirits, that there could be signs of mild poltergeist activity, such as noise, interference with lights and movement of objects. Was there a combination here of a spirit linked to poltergeist activity? On hearing the news that things were getting worse and an "owner" of the poltergeist activity could not be found, I decided to perform a Service of Exorcism. The black figure was the target. I remembered that the official text books did not recommend exorcism for poltergeist activity but was this such or was something more than that involved? I decided there was a disturbing and disruptive presence in the home, so I arrived a second time with my wife and two friends.

I celebrated the Holy Communion with all the staff present and then went on a tour of the house guided by the lady owner praying in every room and commanding in Christ's Name that whatever was disturbing this place would go to its own place, never to return. We returned to the group whom we left, having asked them to pray while we were out of the room and concluded the Service with the Lord's Prayer, an act of dedication and the blessing.

It was a joy to see the relief on their faces when we took our leave. I made one or two calls after that to inquire how things were. Things had returned to normal. The house was at peace and the black figure was not seen again.

Conclusion

Many books have been written about the paranormal from a Christian viewpoint. For those who want to pursue the subject further, I recommend a book by Francis McNutt entitled: "Deliverance from evil spirits" (Publisher Hodder and Stoughton). The author has had wide experience of ministering to people in many countries, including the United States of America where he lives. He has come face to face with human suffering caused by the presence of evil spirits which has required the exercise of the Ministry of Deliverance.

Francis McNutt is a priest of the Roman Catholic Church and approaches this subject with sensitivity and care. It is obvious that he has studied and experienced it extensively and yet the book is very readable, practical and of value to Church leaders who want to help those who may need to be set free from spiritual oppression.

Another scholarly and well researched book is by an Anglican priest, entitled: "Deliver us from evil" (Publisher Darton, Longman & Todd). The author is John Richard who took a year's sabbatical to write the book. Its sub-title is "An introduction to the demonic dimension in pastoral care". It covers a wide range of paranormal activity. Its only drawback for busy people is that it is very detailed and may prove to be more useful as a book of reference.

Other books that are worth reading on the subject are: "Spiritual Warfare" by Michael Harper and "I believe in Satan's Downfall" by Michael Green (Both published by Hodder and Stoughton).

If I have succeeded in persuading some Church leaders and pastors to take the subject of the paranormal more seriously, without "going over the top" and over emphasising it, I will have accomplished what I set out to do. It has not been my intention to turn anyone into a demon hunter or a ghostbuster. Paranormal phenomena are rare but not, perhaps, as rare as we think.